The Treasures of Roberto Cofresí

Black Eagle of the Seas

by

Lubos Kordac

The Treasures of Roberto Cofresí

Published by:
Signum Ops, 435 Nora Ave., Merritt Island, Florida 32952.

ISBN 978-1523477036

Library of Congress Catalog-in-Publication data:
Kordac, Lubos
The Treasures of Roberto Cofresí

All photos by the author unless otherwise noted.

First Edition, Revsion Two, January 27, 2016

Dedications

Dedicated to my lovely wife Ysabel, who has always supported me in my adventures and whenever possible, joins me in my search for the treasures of Cofresí.

Roberto Cofresí, although a pirate, was an extraordinary man in many ways. During his lifetime he helped many of his fellow countrymen, and continued to be an inspirational figure to the poor long after his death. I, myself, am a proof of this inspiration. I believe that in each legend there is a grain of the truth, and I decided to go for it. Like the Scottish national hero, Robert the Bruce once said - "Try, if you do not succeed, try again, and again, until you get it..."

Roberto Cofresí Ramírez de Arellano, the Black Prince of the Caribbean, Black Eagle of the Seas, THANK YOU!

I will never forget you...

Table of Contents

Chapter One

The difference between pirates, corsairs, and buccaneers

There is a common misconception that all of those intrepid characters sailing the seas under the black flag of the skull and cross bones, plundering treasure from merchant ships of all nationalities, were pirates. This statement is not true and it is very important for students of history to know the difference between a pirate, a corsair, and a buccaneer.

The Spanish Crown wanted the entire New World territory with its immense riches only for themselves, but, of course, that was not acceptable to other European nations at that time — especially England, France, Portugal and Holland. The first French assault on Spanish merchant ships sailing from Santo Domingo, carrying valuable sugar cane from Hispaniola, occurred near the Canary Islands as early as 1522. This attack was led by the French "sea thief", Jean Fleury, who captured the Spanish vessel without difficulty, taking her to a French port and selling the cargo for a considerable sum. Shortly after that, in 1528, the first French corsairs invaded the New World. They sacked the small coastal city of San German in today's Puerto Rico. Exploiting the ongoing hostilities between France and Spain, several French adventurers obtained the "corso" patent that allowed them to attack and plunder Spanish ships and towns in the New World beginning in 1537. They plundered the prosperous Spanish town of Compostela de Azua on the southern coast of Hispaniola Island, and they successfully assaulted and burned the town of Santiago de Cuba in 1554. La Habana was sacked in 1555. These attacks were led by a famous Frenchman, Francois Leclerc, nicknamed Pata de Palo (Pegleg). The first English ship arrived in the vicinity of Santo Domingo in 1527 and shortly after that the English presence in the Caribbean was permanent.

The three most successful English pirates operating in this area were Sir Francis Drake, who captured and burned most of Santo Domingo in 1586, accompanied by his uncle, John Hawkins, and Sir Walter Raleigh. The Spanish, weakened by eternal warfare on the European continent, were furious with their neighbors in regards to this maritime hostility, but they could do little about it. The Spaniards elected to call any vessel, aside from their own sailing in the New World, a "pirate" vessel, as all foreign vessels were considered a threat to Spanish commerce. The Spanish did not split hairs; in their view, there was no difference between a corsair, a pirate, or a buccaneer. As defined by historian Don Cayetano Armando Rodriguez, pirates and filibusters were common bandits that operated on their own in times of war or peace. Their only goal was looting.

The term "corsair" was given to an armed ship, especially during times of war, used to attack enemy ships with the special permission of the government under whose flag they were sailing. This written permission, issued on a special parchment, was called a "corso", which is the root of the term "corsair." The corsairs served as an auxiliary navy of any country issuing a given corso and those corsairs had to follow the orders of the their sponsor. When the hostilities between two nations ended, a "ban", or "prohibition of military action" against ships of a former enemy, was issued. Corsair ships then lost their legal permission to attack and plunder the enemy's ships, and if these corsair ships continued their maritime attacks, they came to be outcasts. As such they were generally called pirates or filibusters and were often pursued by their own sponsoring authorities. This was, for example, the case of the famous Captain William Kidd, whose hidden treasure has been sought by dozens of adventurers for more than 300 years. William Kidd, who was originally issued a "corso" patent to attack and plunder ships of England's enemies, especially the French in the Indian Ocean, became a pirate after the truce between these two nations was signed. He was finally caught and hanged in London.

The term "buccaneer" deserves a little more explanation, considering that one of the most famous characters wreaking havoc on the Spanish Main was Sir Henry Morgan. The island of Hispaniola was the first island of the New World to prosper under Spanish rule, and it was also to the first to decline under Spanish rule once conquistadors had conquered Mexico and Peru. The population of this island (sometimes also called the "Island of Santo Domingo") decreased drastically. The main export of the small Spanish community of settlers who remained there was principally leather, but leather alone could not maintain the economy. In order to survive, the inhabitants were forced to trade with merchants of other nations, knowing that such trade was considered by Spanish authorities as illegal. This illegal commerce became very popular in short order, especially on the northern coast of Hispaniola. The Spanish Crown was affected by the loss of business in that region and subsequently sent a small army to burn down all the cities on the entire northern coast of Hispaniola, with an eye toward ending the illegal commerce once for all. This occurred in 1605 and the remaining Spanish settlers were forced to move to the south side of the island, or to the midland mountainous region.

About 25 years later a small group of adventurers, principally of English and French origin, were forced by Spanish authorities to abandon the neighboring island of St. Kitts. They sailed north till they spotted the completely desolate shore of Hispaniola. Seeking a location for long-term settlement, where they could obtain enough food and fresh water, they considered the northern coast of Hispaniola as an almost ideal place for this purpose, so they decided to stay. There were many wild herds of cattle on the island, providing an opportunity to trade fresh meat and leather with ships of various European nations sailing along the coast. From the native inhabitants the adventurers also learned how to smoke fresh meat properly. This technique called "barbecue" today, was known as "boucan" in those days, as originally pronounced by the French. The term "buccaneer" is the English version of the same word.

Over time the demand for smoked meat increased and with it, the logical decrease in raw product as wild pigs and cattle - once plentiful - were hunted with greater frequency. Subsequently, the buccaneers found themselves without work or a means of supporting themselves. Some of them turned to agriculture and planted tobacco, but the majority were not given to domesticity and began searching for alternate means of survival. They found it at sea, imitating their former customers, the pirates.

"Buccaneer" is a term sometimes used as a substitute for the word "pirate" who attacked and plundered both Spanish ships and Spanish settlements in the New World in the 17th and 18th century. But a buccaneer was not any common pirate. The buccaneers were a defined cultural group of specific people that lived according to special laws and traditions. They were united by their hatred of Roman Catholicism and Imperial Spain. They called themselves the "Brethren of the Coast" and they had their own code of conduct, their own code of honor, their own legendary history, and their own independent style of governance.

In the beginning the pirates and buccaneers attacked merchant ships that sailed without escorts. Thereafter, with increased organization and burgeoning membership, these rovers began to attack entire fleets of vessels, and eventually, acted as invading armies as

entire countries and cities became their prey. The buccaneers who participated in these adventures could be identified by their common costumes, weapons, and rules of conduct, all of which they shared previously as they lived and hunted together. Quite often, these buccaneers would return to Hispaniola for fresh supplies, and to smoke

Left: Sir John Hawkins

meat, as was their habit. The money they looted was quickly spent on wine, and women, and exhausted of cash, they would repeat their cycle of crime on the high seas.

New World hostilities between European kingdoms began early on in the colonial epic of the Western Hemisphere. The actual outbreak of international warfare in the theater of the Spanish Main was piqued by an incident between the English and the Spanish at the Bay of San Juan de Ulua in 1567. The English "merchant", read "smuggler", John Hawkins was anchored in the bay with his fleet when the Spanish fleet with the new governor of New Spain, Martin Henríquez, sailed into the harbor. Despite Hawkins' claims of simple commercial interest, the Spanish, without warning, attacked his fleet on the spot and only two Englishmen escaped; Hawkins himself, and his nephew, Francis Drake. When the pair returned to England in 1569, the tale of this incident evoked the rage of public insult to the English nation and it was taken as a pretext to initiate immediate political and military reprisals against Spain.

Mutual hostilities between British pirates, French corsairs, and the Spanish that started in 1569 continued throughout the Caribbean almost till the first half of the 19th century.

Roberto Cofresí Ramírez de Arellano was practically the last real pirate in the Caribbean. He was preceded in his area of operation by other more famous personages, and some lesser, such as Pierre le Grand, a French captain who, using a small boat manned with twenty eight hands, managed to capture the flag ship of the Spanish fleet in front of Cape Tiburon on the south coast of Hispaniola. The area was considered a rich target for plunder as hundreds of vessels plied the lanes annually, traveling to and fro with cargo bound for, or collected from Spanish colonies in the New World. It is little wonder that Hispaniola attracted so many men with a desire to obtain wealth quickly... through commerce or otherwise.

Those men who opted for plunder include the likes of the very cruel pirate, Bartolome the Portuguese, famous for his numerous escapes from Spanish prisons in the New World; Pierre Francois; Rock the Brazilian, who was a Dutchman that spent his youth with his parents in Brazil; Miguel el Vasco; Lewis Scot, who was the first to attack a Spanish settlement on land; Juan David, who specialized in attacking ships coming to or from Nicaragua; Tributor, a French corsair; Montbars the Exterminator with his terrible war axe; Manweld, who made several raids in Yucatan; Pierre le Picard; Bras de Fer; Laurant; Van Horn; Grammont; Jungue; Bronage; Le Sage; Jack Bannister; Carlos Roinel; Blackbeard; Henry Morgan; and we cannot forget, of course, to mention Sir Francis Drake.

In the 17th and 18th centuries, pirates, corsairs and other similar adventurers formed their principal Caribbean base of operation in the city of Port Royal, in Jamaica. Thanks to the stolen treasures brought there by the pirates, the city soon became one of the richest of the New World. A huge earthquake, followed by tidal waves, ended this prosperity once and for all in 1692. Unlike the pirates and corsairs, the buccaneers had always based themselves on Tortuga Island, which continues to bear that name even today. This island is actually in Haitian territory and it is located approximately 60 nautical miles from Montecristi on the northern coast of the Dominican Republic. The island's waters are littered with the remains of sunken ships and there are allegedly many buried treasures to be found on the island itself. The island appears, from a distance, to resemble a turtle, thus the name "Tortuga", which is the Spanish term for turtle.

Left: Henry Morgan

All of these pirates, corsairs, and buccaneers were active in the Caribbean for almost three hundred years, plundering, looting and terrorizing the public at land and on the high seas. The golden era of piracy in the Caribbean ended with the Black Prince of the Pirates, also known as the Black Eagle of the Caribbean, Roberto Cofresí de Ramírez y Arellano.

Above: part of the city of Port Royal sank into the ocean during an earthquake in 1692.

Who among us has not seen a movie about pirates attacking Spanish galleons loaded with gold, silver, and emeralds somewhere in the Caribbean? Who among us has not read a book on this subject, and who among us has not dreamt, at least once, of finding a pirate treasure? Pirates are romantic characters who inspire the images of buried treasure, and strong men surrounded by beautiful women; men who not only satisfied their own lust for wealth, but who, on occasion, fought for their own ideals, supporting their less fortunate, suppressed countrymen. These stories and fictional movie plots are far from the truth, with at least one exception, that being the legend of Roberto Cofresí y Ramírez de Arellano, the last real pirate of the Caribbean, a true legend that has survived for almost 200 years.

Roberto Cofresí was active as a pirate for very short time — just for four years, but he was extremely successful in his maritime enterprises — he and his small crew of friends managed to assault and plunder more than sixty ships during this short period, a fact supported by historical proof. He was a hero to the ordinary people and hundreds of families all over the islands of Puerto Rico and Hispaniola. He was one of them, always returning from his successful ocean raids, and sharing his booty with the local people.

The author before the treasure hunt, above, and after the hunt, below.

Little wonder that they loved to help him by being his eyes and ears throughout the region.

Cofresí always declared that any crew of a ship that he boarded would simply be locked in the storeroom if they offered no resistance. He would then depart, doing them no harm, once he'd looted his prize. There is only a single documented case of barbarity by the Cofresí gang... the captain of a captured ship slapped Cofresí with his leather glove. Cofresí had the captured crew stripped naked, tied to the masts in the burning sun, and he had the captain hung upside down from the bowsprit.

Some authors claim Cofresí was a corsair, operating under the authority of a corso awarded by the Gran Columbia Republic, but this is not true. This confusion arises from the little known fact that Cofresí did a short stint on one corsair ship for a short time, but he decided to operate as a pirate early on in his dangerous, but highly profitable profession.

Some of the more famous pirates, corsairs, and buccaneers are known to have buried one or more treasures. The more celebrated examples would include Captain Kidd, Francis Drake, or Henry Morgan. Kidd allegedly hid secret maps of his island treasure location in hidden compartments in a desk, found decades later after his death. The maps were found, but the island and the treasure remain elusive. Kidd's last words on the gallows were: "If you hang me, you will never find my treasure..." A similar scenario occurred with the execution of pirate Olivier Levasseur, who tossed a coded message into the spectator mob at his hanging while he bellowed: "Find my treasure, he who may understand it!" To this day, treasure hunters continue to break the code and find Levasseur's treasure.

Francis Drake, having looted the Spanish galleon Cacafuegos along the coast of Ecuador, found that his own vessel the Golden Hind could not possibly carry all the treasure he'd found, so he supposedly buried some of it on a small island known today as Isla de la Plata. Some silver bars have been found in a bay of this island, years ago, but no treasure has been found on the island itself.

Henry Morgan sacked Panama City and is rumored to have buried a large part of his booty somewhere in the area so as to avoid sharing it with his French confederates. After becoming governor of Jamaica, he never returned to Panama to dig it up because he was quite wealthy and had no need of the spare cash! This treasure, searched for by many adventurers in the mean while has never been found... Morgan took the location with him to his grave.

Roberto Cofresí 's thrilling life story is filled with adventure, but the adrenaline really starts to flow when you consider his buried treasures! He left behind many rumors of buried treasure, but unlike his compatriots who might have buried one or two treasures, Cofresí buried many of them! He is supposed to have buried treasure in many places around the shores of Hispaniola, Mona Island, and Puerto Rico.

At the beginning of the 19th century, there were no banks or financial institutions that would deal with a wanted man, so it became necessary for Roberto Cofresí to stash some of his loot in various places, ever mindful of that eventual "rainy day" always looming on the horizon for any man of his profession. This certainly makes perfect sense to me. Having read all the available books on Roberto Cofresí, visiting all the noted locations, examining all of the relevant documentation and newspaper articles, hearing all of the local lore of the fishermen, and generally investigating Roberto Cofresí for more than ten years, I could assemble a list of potential treasure burials numbering thirty in total that could be found on Hispaniola and Mona Island. Some of these can be found on Puerto Rico as well.

One might smile and dismiss these stories with a wave of one's hand and claim them to be nonsense, but, during the last fifty years three treasures have been found on Hispaniola and another on Mona Island, all of which were located as Cofresí described, and all of which contained the goods as described by Cofresí. So I asked myself if the other legendary buried treasures of Roberto Cofresí should not also exist? And I decided to found out for myself, regardless of the repeated warning from history that those who might find these treasures shall be followed by bad luck and madness for the rest of his life.

The father – black sheep of the family

The family of Roberto Cofresí y Ramírez de Arellano originated in Italy. His father was Fancesco von Kupferschein, and he was born in the Italian harbor town of Trieste, the son of one of the respected directors of the police department, Giovanni Giuseppe Stanislao von Kupferschein. The family immigrated to Italy from Austria and because immigrants were required by Italian authorities to adopt Italian sounding names, they were known there by the surname of Confersin.

The first known ancestor of the family was Cristoforo Kupferschein, who officially received the family coat of arms with a crest and diploma from the King of Bohemia and Hungary, Ferdinand I who eventually became the King of the Holy Roman Empire. Cristoforo was awarded the coat of arms in Prague, which today is the capital of the Czech Republic, on the 3rd of December of 1549. Cristoforo then went to Kaernten in Austria, where he later died and his sons eventually settled in Trieste, Italy. They were, no doubt, a noble family and in short order became a part of the higher class of this important city. One of the boys, Fenicio, the grandfather of Francesco von Kupferschein, was recognized by the government of this harbor city for his work as a principal tax collector in Trieste.

So, the Kupferscheins were, undoubtedly, respected nobility in the city of Trieste but Francesco von Kupferschein, an only son, was the black sheep of the family. He was born on the 12th of July of 1751 and he had two sisters, Maria Anna Gioseffa and Margarita Gioseffa von Kupferschein, both being respected ladies. In 1776 Franz (or Francesco), worked as a norary clerk in the criminal court of Trieste, as did his brother-in-law, Domenico Dolcetti, and their friend Josephus Stephani. However, Francesco spent much of his time with his friends, sailors from Muggia, who were rumored to be smugglers, something that was never proven as fact. In one instance, Francesco, along with four "friends" was surprised by a coworker from the notary office, Josephus Stephani, in the middle of the night inside the town walls at the exact moment the group was transporting a huge amount of contraband into the city. Francesco simply could not risk the family name being jeopardized by any loose talk of Stephani. In an instant, it was decided that Stephani must be killed. This occurred on the 31st of July of 1778, just a few days after Francesco had celebrated his 27th birthday.

EL ESCUDO DE LA FAMILIA KUPFERSCHEIN

Above: Coat of arms of the Kupferschein family

The five conspirators threw Stephani to the ground and held him there. At first they considered drowning him in the sea but then decided that they did not have the time to do that. After a short discussion they decided to beat poor Josephus to death with wooden clubs. That done, they left the corpse behind the ruins of an old building and quickly smuggled their contraband into the city. They thought that they had killed Stephani but they were wrong. The next morning Josephus was found unconscious but still alive and he was immediately taken to the hospital. Before he died he told authorities what had happened the previous night and he accused Francesco von Kupferschein along with his four friends of trying to murder him. The dreadful news reached the Kupferschein family in short order and they decided that Francesco must leave the city at once. The four sailors left hurriedly the next morning to hide in a remote part of Macedonia, but Francesco, having knowledge of foreign languages, preferred to leave for Barcelona, where the Kupferscheins had some relatives.

He was extremely worried, because it was clear that, apart from official persecution, the family of the murdered Josephus would seek vengeance as was customary in those days. On the 8th of August of 1778, Francesco left for Barcelona aboard a small ship in search of a new life, a few days before Trieste authorities issued an arrest order for the murder of Josephus Stephani. Francesco's family gave him enough money so that he would avoid any financial shortfall during his escape.

For the next six months Francesco Giuseppe Fortunato von Kupferschein had a very nice stay in Barcelona - he had no need to work because he occasionally received more money from his family in Trieste - so he just enjoyed his lazy, social life in this huge Catalan city. But the sweet days abruptly ended for Francesco in the middle of 1779 with the news that the family of Josephus had discovered his whereabouts and had sent one of the family members to kill him, fulfilling the promise of vengeance. The person selected to kill Francesco was Joachim Bonifacios Stefani, a brother of the murder victim. Because of his physical appearance Joachim was nicknamed "The Bull", a moniker he deserved.

Joachim knew Francesco from school and in those days they were friends. Joachim Steffani, apart from his frightening appearance was also a renowned swordsman and one of the best knife throwers in Trieste. To make the things worse, the news of Joachim's threat was delivered to Francesco by one of his own cousins who happened to see "The Bull" at the Barcelona harbor that very same day. The Kupferschein family quickly determined that Francesco should leave as quickly as possible for the New World to avoid an untimely death.

Having no desire to push his luck any further, on the following day Francesco Kupferschein left for Seville and from there he bid farewell to the Old World as he boarded a Spanish merchant ship bound for the Caribbean, more precisely for the city of Santo Domingo in Hispaniola.

Life in Santo Domingo was not so social like that in Barcelona or Trieste but much quieter. He had no immediate family members to support him here so Francesco decided to try his luck in the army and before long he enlisted in the Spanish Batallon Fijo of Santo Domingo. His height of almost six and a half feet, blond hair, blue eyes and white skin, coupled with his martial status as a single male soon made him a target of almost all the ladies in the city. Francesco was happy again and completely forgot the murderous shadow of "The Bull".

But his fate changed abruptly once more. Francesco's battalion was dispatched to the borderlands of the Spanish colony adjoining the French portion where a surprise conflict had erupted. So instead of enjoying a comfortable life in Santo Domingo, Francesco was now patrolling a small border town called Dajabon. It was here that problems with his surname began. People simply could not pronounce the name Kupferschein and so they started to call him Cufersin, Cofresí nos, Confersin or Confercin. Finally the name that was most often used came to be Cofresí. In documents from that period the name can be also be found as Kuppersein, Coupperseing or Koffressi. On the birth certificate of Roberto, his son (our famous pirate), his surname was written as "Cofresír" and on his death certificate he was cited as "Cufresir". Doña Rosalía Cofresí de Silva, says that her father, a cousin of Roberto Cofresí, used to sign his name as "Coufferssing."

After several months Francesco received orders to relocate to the garrison in San Juan de la Majuana. Here he met his future wife, Maria Germana Ramirez de Arellano y Segarra. A resident of Puerto Rico, she was visiting San Juan de la Majuana for a few days accompanying her father who'd arrived there for the funeral of one of their relatives, a former resident of San Juan de la Majuana. One evening Frencesco and Maria danced together... they talked and then parted ways. But they were destined to meet again.

A few months after this encounter Francesco received interesting news that there was small colony of families from Trieste in newly established coastal town of Cabo Rojo on the neighboring island of Puerto Rico, and beautiful girl, whom he met months ago was living there — by coincidence — as well.

Knowing that a ship had arrived several days earlier from Seville carrying a huge man called "The Bull", the very same man who was seeking him out, Francesco must now make another life changing decision. Joachim Stephanie was told that Francesco was serving as a soldier in Dajabon, and he departed for that village immediately to carry out his mission of revenge.

So Francesco quickly decided to resign from his military career and in a hurry packed for a journey to the neighboring island of Puerto Rico. Later he learned that "The Bull" lingered during his trip for one or two days in Santiago de los Caballeros, a large city in the middle of the island. He met a girl there and he immediately fell in love with her. Stephani completely forgot his murderous mission, married the girl and settled in Santiago forever. By that time Francisco Cofresí (Kupferschein) had already arrived at Cabo Rojo.

In 1986 a Setphanie descendant was located in the Dominican city of Santiago de los Caballeros. I contacted Mr. Hector (Bullo) Stephani by letter, but he never answered. Obviously the family remained there for more than 200 years.

Francesco managed to buy a piece of land in Cabo Rojo and built a modest house there. In the autumn of 1872 he finished it and started looking for the girl he had met that fateful night in San Juan de la Majuana. It did not take long to find her and he proposed marriage, which was gladly accepted by her and also by her family. Nobody knew in that small coastal town of Puerto Rico that there had been a trial in Trieste in January of 1780, where Francesco von Kupferschein was officially condemned in absentia for the murder of his friend.

Francesco (or Francisco) Cofresí lived happily with his new wife María Germana Ramírez de Arrellano y Segarra in their small house and on the 21st of June of 1785 María gave a birth to their first daughter, Juana Cofresí y Ramírez de Arrellano. Two years later, on the 25th of March of 1787 their first son, Juan Francisco, was born, followed by Ignacio, born on the 16th of September of 1789. Finally their last child was brought on the world as Roberto Cofresí y Ramírez de Arrellano, who was born on the 12th of June of 1791, and baptized on the 27th of June of the same year.

Four years later Francisco went for a pleasant boat ride along the coast of Cabo Rojo with his wife María. The children were at home. The day was peaceful and quiet until the couple was approached by an English brig. The English crew tortured Francisco, raped María and then quickly left. She was later found, taken to the hospital and she survived but she could not live with the shame, sadness and pain from the fate of her husband. The mother of Roberto Cofresí, María Germana y Ramírez de Arrellano, died a few months later, leaving four children behind. Roberto, though only four years old at the time, never forgot this incident and it's said that this was one of the reasons why he later attacked English ships so furiously, showing no mercy to their crews.

Five years later Roberto's father married Maria Sanabria, who was also from Cabo Rojo. Francesco Giuseppe Fortunato von Kupferschein (Cofresí) died on the 29th of September 1814. He was 63 years old and was given a Christian burial in Cabo Rojo.

Chapter Two

Childhood and early years of Roberto Cofresí

Roberto was born in the coastal town of Cabo Rojo, in a very small place called Tujao, close to the actual neighborhood of Puerto Real (according to the baptism book of Cabo Rojo, number 4, folio 31). He was baptized on the 27th of June 1791. There is a theory that the name Tujao was derived from English words for "two houses".

Very little is known about his early childhood. Salvador Brau, who dedicated many years researching the life of Roberto Cofresí, states that Roberto was stubborn, refusing advice of his family and relatives, and continually attracted to the sea. No wonder; Cabo Rojo was an important harbor with many ships coming and going, and a center of smuggling operations.

Little Roberto was four years old when he became motherless. Because his father was very busy trying to support all his children, he did not have enough time to dedicate to his young and very temperamental Roberto. The boy was passed from one relative to another, living here and there for a couple of months. According to many historians, most of the time he lived with his aunt, doña María Merced, in Tujao, close to a place called Joyuda where he was born. He missed his mother and many neighbors did everything possible to console him or entertain him. His father tried to get the best education for all four children, but this proved to be financially impossible. Francisco wanted Roberto to study law, but young Roberto was not interested in anything that was not related to the sea. Nor was he much interested in typical children's games, and if he was not at the cemetery kneeling before the grave of his mother, he preferred to spend his time on the shore watching ships passing by Cabo Rojo.

Many foreigners were attracted to the town over time as smuggling boomed. In 1774 Cabo Rojo was a town of 1,200 inhabitants, 50 % of which were sailors and adventurers from Europe. Roberto soon made friends with several sailors from Pedernales, which was a neighborhood in Cabo Rojo. He dreamed of being captain of his own boat one day and before long, at the age of seven, he was well acquainted with the terminology of sailors; he knew the purpose specific knots, and how to use different ropes and sails. It was at this time when he got his own small sailboat. He proudly called it *El Mosquito* (Some historians use the name of his small boat *Relámpago*, which means *Lightning*).

When he could, Roberto helped his father selling fruits and fish to passing ships. At about the age of seven, he chanced to visit an American merchant ship to sell them his fresh merchandise. The ship had a cargo of sugar. Once aboard, young Roberto noticed that one of the sugar sacks was broken and some sugar had fallen out. He took some and ate it but he was caught by the American captain who gave him a beating and threw him off of his ship. Roberto swore that he would take revenge on any American ships in the future. Some historians mention this episode in Cofresí's life as a milestone in which he decided to become a pirate and attack American ships. Some time later he was sailing with his small sailboat in the bay when an English brigantine ran him over on purpose. He barely made it to shore, swimming furiously, and hearing the laughter of the English sailors, his hatred of any English speaking crew became even more intense.

In 1824, by chance, Roberto came upon the American captain and the same ship upon which he was caught eating sugar as a child. Roberto took his vengeance in full. After he forced the American captain and his crew to transfer all the merchandise to his pirate ship, he locked them in the storeroom and burnt their vessel. The American captain was the only one who died during this incident.

When Roberto was eight years old, he asked his father to allow him to work as a ship's boy aboard of a small merchant ship. Francisco wanted his son to get the best possible training for a decent trade, and refused Roberto's request at first. He hoped Roberto would become lawyer, like he himself had been back in Triest. Roberto was then enrolled in the primary neighborhood school of Guaniqiuilla, but in spite of being an excellent student, young Roberto preferred to spend most of his time on the seashore, or rowing around in his small boat. Seeing this, his father called together the family council of his children, uncles and aunts, and finally decided to send Roberto to the neighboring island of Hispaniola for two or three years to live with relatives in Santo Domingo, where he might get some experience and learn a little more about a seaman's skills.

Several days later a small balandra, the *Milanesa*, under the command of one of Francisco's friends, arrived at Cabo Rojo and Roberto said good-bye to his family. Captain Francisco Brassetti showed him around the ship and after two days under sail they arrived in Santo Domingo. Fortunately, one of Roberto's relatives had a boy named Jose who was the same age as Roberto, and both boys attended the same school the following September where they became fast friends.

Occasionally Roberto's guardians were visited by Eusebio Hernandez, whose wife was a sister of Roberto's mother. Eusebio lived in Samaná and twice a month sailed his small boat, *Las Pascuas,* to Santo Domingo with a cargo of coconuts. Little Roberto was immediately attracted to the personality of his uncle and it did not take long before he convinced Eusebio to take him along on excursions to Samaná.

Time went by quickly and little Roberto Cofresí easily passed all his school exams. On the 22nd of December of 1799, at the age of nine, he boarded *Las Pascuas,* the ship of Eusebio Hernandez, in company with his new friend, Jose, bound for Samaná where the duo planned to spend some free time. The ship sailed between Samaná and Santo Domingo on a regular basis with cargos of dry coconuts from Samaná, while carrying foodstuffs from the capital on the reverse leg of the voyage. This small vessel only had one sailor, Juan

Above: map of Santo Domingo circa 1805, when young Roberto lived in this city

Almeyda, apart from the owner/captain. After his stay in Samana, Roberto asked Eusebio Hernandez if he would accept him as a ship's boy when he finished school the following June. Hernandez agreed.

Note: Much later, Almeyda joined the Cofresí pirate crew.

Working aboard his relative's small barque, Roberto had an opportunity to visit many harbors, both large and small, and the bays throughout the island of Hispaniola. He learned the names of these places, the location of dangerous currents, the rocks and reefs that must be avoided, the cycles of the tides, and the best anchorage/careening locations. Roberto was smart boy and he was eager to learn everything related to the sailor´s trade. The barque always returned home to Samaná, where Eusebio had his house, wife and little boy, Joaquim, who was four years old in 1800. Between voyages, the boys explored the never-ending mangrove channels and lakes in Samaná Bay, and this knowledge of the local geography served Roberto Cofresí well as he evaded his pursuing enemies in the future.

At this time Toussaint Louverture successfully occupied the entire island and he officially declared Hispaniola to be a French territory in 1802. When Louverture, while in the town square in Santo Domingo (today this square is called Columbus Square in the Colonial City — author) proclaimed all Negro slaves on the island to be free, Eusebio Hernández, his first mate, Juan Almeyda, and Roberto Cofresí y Ramírez de Arellano were all three there as well. As history shows, things did not go well for the Negro general. France sent over 60 ships full of soldiers to Samaná and Toussaint Louverture retreated to the western part of the island where, in 1804, he declared the first Negro state in the world we now know as Haiti. The French were issuing "corso patents" to many captains and their crews in order to harass the maritime business routes around the island and for some time Santo Domingo became the ad hoc base for these corsairs. Jose, a cousin of Juan Almeyda, arrived at Samaná one day on board of such a French corsair, the *L' Espliegue*. When Roberto saw this ship, and heard the adventurous tales of the crew-members he could not sleep.

Nine months later a sailor was needed for this particular vessel and this was an opportunity for Roberto Cofresí that he would not miss. He jumped on this opportunity, and thanks to his vast experience shipboard, his physical prowess, and knowledge, the captain of *L' Espliegue*, gladly accepted him as a crewmember. On their first day out of Santo Domingo harbor they successfully attacked and ransacked the Turkish ship *Ankara*.

Many more victims were to follow. When a ship was captured, it was taken back to port and booty was shared with the "authorities". On one such visit, Roberto was introduced to a friend of Captain Cadet, the French corsair, Juan Bart. It seemed that some of Bart's crew had been injured during his last attack of a hapless victim at sea, and he was in need of replacements. Bart turned to Cadet for help and before he knew it, Roberto was enlisted, or rather, loaned to Bart while the injured crew were mending on shore. It was difficult to turn down a "request" from Juan Bart. Bart's ship, *La Bella Marsellesa* prowled the southern coast of the island where she overcame many American merchant ships. When not under sail, La Bella Marsellesa would hide away in coves of the island of Alto Velo, Bart's main base of operations. In the following years, Roberto Cofresí also made use of the same island for the same purposes. Bart frequented Isla Beata, an island close to Alto Velo, where wood for charcoal was plentiful, as were the turtles that served as mainstay protein.

At this time in history, Pope Alexander VI had a great bias for the catholic kingdoms of Portugal and Spain, resulting in his apportionment of the New World between those two estates. France was forgotten. France would not suffer such papal insults and intended to get her share of whatever treasures the New World had to offer, therefore, the plunder of her adversary's ships was the order of the day. Subsequently, French corsairs and French pirates were plentiful in the Antilles.

Early in 1808, *La Bella Marsellesa* docked in Santo Domingo. Roberto visited relatives there and on this occasion he was given a letter sent to him by his father. The letter asked that Roberto return to Puerto Rico as soon as possible as his father was seriously ill. By now, Roberto Cofresí and Juan Bart had become fast friends, and Roberto was given leave of Bart's pirate enterprise, where upon he returned to his hometown in Puerto Rico.

Seeing his son once again temporarily improved the health of Roberto's father. Roberto's father pleaded with him to take up a trade on land as a farmer or merchant, but Roberto would have none of that. His hot blood drew him to a life as a marauder at sea, and a dream to obtain a corso patent of his own. For a short while, Roberto remained at home in support of his father's delicate health, but he was unhappy as he was trapped on land. On September 29th, 1814, Francisco Kupferschein-Cofresí called his son to his bed for the last time, pleading with him to remain on dry land. Roberto refused, and on the following day, his father died.

Many colonies in South America began struggling for independence from Spain in 1811. The flame of revolution spread far and wide; its heat radiated throughout the Caribbean with consequences in Puerto Rico, Hispaniola, Jamaica, and Cuba, where surrounding shipping lanes became plagued by upstart corsairs of the newly hatched South American republics. Merchant shipping was threatened daily and maritime traffic slowed to a halt with the captains of Cabo Rojo especially fearful of putting to sea. Fierce naval battles raged all around the Spanish Main. No ship was safe from the depredations of the ex-Spanish colonists. Even fishermen found themselves under threat. Slaves began escaping to sea where some might sail to freedom, while others were re-captured by the Spanish authorities, or lost to the deep. All of these factors played their part in the career of the young Roberto Cofresí.

Three short months after the death of his father, Roberto Cofresí de Ramírez y Arellano married Juanita Creitoff Hoevertz on the 14th of January, 1815. He'd fallen in love with her a few months earlier, and although she was only fourteen years old, Roberto did not want to wait any longer for their nuptials. She was from respected family that had migrated to the Caribbean from Holland. Her father had died in Curazao. When Roberto asked Juanita's mother for permission to marry her daughter, he was pleasantly surprised when permission was granted. Indeed, the entire town celebrated the marriage, thinking that, at last, that Roberto's wild temperament might, at last, be calmed, and that he might take up a steady, respectable trade.

Having no money, the young couple took up residence with Juanita's mother, Juana. Several months after the marriage, disaster struck when the house burned to the ground. The fire resulted in more and more debt for the family, but despite their poverty, church archives indicate that Roberto paid his communal duties regardless. There is an entry confirming that Roberto Cofresí paid the modest sum of 17 maravedis to the church priest in 1818. A year later he paid 5 reales. The Cofresís lived in a modest wood house with Juanita's mother until 1819. During that time their happiness was overshadowed by the death of Roberto's sister, Juana, who died of tuberculosis on November 19th, 1815, at the age of 30. Roberto's brother-in-law, German Colberg, died two years later on February 20th, 1817. German was 33 years old at the time of his death.

Though poor, the skilled and clever Roberto began making friends with the influential families of Cabo Rojo. The young couple lived happily in their modest house, and on June 7th, 1819 their first-born son, Juan Cofresí de Ramírez y Arellano, came into this world. On April 6th, 1820, just prior to Juan's first birthday, he became ill with a lung disease and died shortly thereafter. Following his son's death, Roberto made a living as a sailor aboard a vessel delivering victuals to Tallaboa from the port of Cabo Rojo. Being good at his job, he was promoted to captain of the merchant transport *Ramona*.

On the 17th of August 1821, Juanita gave birth to another child, this time a girl, given the name Bernardina. (Actually, she was the only child who would survive. The couple had one more son,

Francisco Matías, who was born on the 24th of February, 1824, while Roberto Cofresí was on the high seas, but the boy was born with some illness and he died just two weeks later). Disaster struck once again within a few months when Roberto fell out with the owner of the *Ramona*, and Roberto was fired from his good job as captain of the vessel. For the next year, Roberto tried to find work so that he might support his baby daughter and wife, but to no avail. The economical balance of the entire Caribbean was thrown off by the political tensions in that region. The Cofresí's situation became desperate. The shortages of food and money, the lack of industry and commerce, coupled with the poor administration of the island by corrupt Spanish officials had brought about malaise and despair throughout the region. Young men, without jobs or hope, began robbing and stealing to make their way. Murders became common in the neighborhood of Cabo Rojo, Yauco, and Pedernales, the community where Roberto lived. That at least three of these desperados became crewmen aboard Cofresí's pirate ships later on has been confirmed... Juan de los Reyes, nicknamed "El Indio", Francisco Ramos, and José "Pepe" Cartagena.

According to historian Walter Cardona Bonet, Roberto Cofresí colluded with a group of his young friends in the assault of the small neighborhood of Yauco, where they stole some merchandise that they later sold. By the end of June 1821, Roberto and his confederates were caught and imprisoned. He was in jail at San Germán during the months of July and August of 1821 waiting for trial. On the 17th of August of the same year, his wife gave birth to his daughter, Bernardina, and authorities permitted Roberto to visit his wife and newly born child. Without hesitation, he took this opportunity to escape. The mayor of San Germán, Pascario Cardona, fired the judge who gave permission to Roberto to leave jail and he issued a warrant for Roberto Cofresí as an absconder. Walter Cardona is the only historian who mentions this episode. All other Cofresí biographers imply that Roberto was simply unemployed and living with his wife in their domicile during this period. At the time, both of Roberto's brothers, Ignacio and Francisco, were making a modest living as sailors. Ignacio managed to become captain of a small merchant sailboat, the *Avispa*, in 1823. Francisco, through his own connections, became co-owner of the ship *Monserrate* in 1824. (There is record of Roberto serving as a sailor for a short time under his brother Ignacio aboard *Avispa* as well).

Toward the end of 1821, Roberto Cofresí had made a decision to join the ranks of the privateers by accepting a position aboard the *Carmen*, a vessel solely devoted to the theft of merchandise on the high seas. He told his wife of his plan. He was desperate, his family was starving, and he could think of no other way to make money. But, with some reserve, he and his wife thought better of his new "profess-sion" until after they had baptized their little daughter. Even though they were poor, they managed to convince a respected pillar of the community, Bernardo Pavon Davila to become the Godfather of their child. Notably, Davila became the mayor of Cabo Rojo in 1822.

After assuming his new duties aboard the *Carmen*, Roberto visited his family sporadically over the following months, but with each visit he brought money. Never ashore for more than a day, Roberto eventually provided his family with enough cash to purchase a modest house.

At the close of 1822, Roberto left the *Carmen* when offered the post of first mate aboard the much larger ship, *Escipion*, then commanded by Jose Ramon Torres. The *Escipion* had a crew of thirty men, and carried two cannon. The vessel was owned by one of Roberto's relatives, José María Ramírez de Arellano, who was mayor of the neighboring city of Mayaguez.

Jose had procured a corso patent with the expectation of making respectable profits. Roberto made several trips on board of *Escipion*, but in June 1823, during the assault of the American merchantman Otter, he suffered an injury to his hand, which put him at home his wound healed. After two months he was ready to resume his post aboard the *Escipion*, but found that the roster for both the *Carmen* and *Escipion* were full. During his stay on shore, the politics on Puerto Rico had completely changed, and there were to be no further issues of corso patents. Futhermore, existing patents were to expire without renewal. Roberto was unemployed once more, with all of his previous earnings spent. Subsequently, Roberto now decided that he would form his own pirate crew.

Ships of Roberto Cofresí

Confusion reigns when discussing the names of the ships Cofresí used along with the date ranges these various boats were under his command. While a small boy, Roberto allegedly had his own rowboat, which he named *El Mosquito*. When he and his comrades stole their first ship and sailed it to Samana Bay where they repainted it, the stolen vessel was supposedly named the *El Mosquete*. Roberto renamed it *El Mosquito*, in homage to his original rowboat.

Meantime, Puerto Rican historian Tapia states that Roberto's first pirate ship was the *Santo Cristo* and, using *Santo Cristo*, he attacked the merchant ship *El Mosquito*, which he seized for his own use as a raider, keeping that ship for some time. According to Tapia, Cofresí always wanted a ship that belonged to Juan Bautista Pieretti, the *La Anguila*.

Another author, Toro Soler, claims that Cofresí 's first pirate ship was the *Relámpago* (*Lightning*). It was thirty feet long, eight feet wide and it allowed him to enter the most shallow mangrove channels giving his pursuers the slip. Vicente Pales Matos claims that Roberto used the pirate ship bearing the name *Maria Cristina*.

Another author by the name of Camacho stated that Cofresí's first ship was called *Delia*. Using this ship Cofresí attacked and looted another merchant ship, the *Eva*, that suited him better; so he left *Delia* and used the *Eva* for his pirate activities for some time. Then he went to Cuba where he bought the ship of his dreams, *El Aguila Negra*. He lost this ship in front of the small fishing harbor of Puerto Juanita on the northern coast.

Based on the accounts of authors and historians, such as Vivas Maldonado, Huyke, Coll y Toste, Eugenio Gonzáles, Rodríguez Escudero and Ibern, the most famous ship of Roberto Cofresí was the *Ana*, which he supposedly bought from Toribio Centeno in 1824.

Roberto Cofresí was, for a short time, alleged to have made use of a merchant ship, the *Neptune*, he'd looted earlier. This occurred shortly before his last fight at sea.

There is confusion regarding the name of the ship Cofresí used in his last battle at sea. Some say he was aboard the *Ana*; others claim that it was the *Neptune,* and others state he was on board of *El Mosquito.*

Given these circumstances, it is very difficult to determine which ship he scuttled in Samaná Bay in front of Punta Gorda, while being pursued by Spanish ships.

There are three names most frequently attributed to Roberto Cofresí's ships - *Ana, El Mosquito,* and *El Aguila Negra. El Aguila Negra* was lost in front of Puerto Juanita, there is no doubt about it, so it could be that one of the other two remaining ships was sunk in front of Punta Gorda. But, who knows?

The escape from jail

Transported by prison ship to Santo Domingo, Cofresí and Gonzáles were jailed at the infamous Torre del Homenaje in the fort of Ozama. Among the other prisoners in Cofresí 's cell were sailors of the corsair Escipion, accused of piracy. There were also some political prisoners accused of conspiracy against the Haitian government. Shortly after his imprisonment, on the 3rd of October 1824, Cofresí was condemned to six years in prison for acts of piracy, and his friend, Ricardo Gonzáles, was given two years in prison for the same reason. But Roberto Cofresí y Ramírez de Arellano was lucky again. The commander of the Haitian military forces in Santo Domingo, Colonel Henri Etienne Desgrottes, was also in charge of the fort of Ozama, and the colonel did not want harm the Dominican legend. Shortly after the trial he arranged a means of escape for Cofresí and three of his friends. The colonel's escape plan was secretly approved by General Borguella, who sent for Roberto Cofresí a few days after his trial and told him that they would help him escape if he would swear that he would never return to Santo Domingo. Of course Roberto Cofresí agreed!

A soldier, Manuel Daniel, was on guard the next night at the cell of Cofresí. This soldier was suspected of wanting to leave the Haitian army and return to his native village in Puerto Rico. Desgrottes promised to fulfill his wish if he would help Cofresí and his two by joining them in their escape from the prison. The Haitian govern-

Above: Ozama fort today. The tower served as prison for centuries and remains unchanged since Roberto Cofresí was held captive there.

ment did not want harm the legendary pirate because he was pursued by Spanish authorities, the same Spanish that were the enemies of the Hatians. In the middle of the night they descended from the prison tower on a rope to the banks of the Ozama River, where a small boat with some food and a pair of oars awaited them. The five fugitives silently rowed out the river's mouth into the open sea unnoticed by the slumbering public. They knew that the next morning at 7 o'clock the escape would be discovered and that military units would be sent to search for them.

Once they passed Boca Chica, they went ashore and followed a tiny path in the underbrush towards the small fishing village of Mosquito y Sol where Cofresí had many friends. Upon arrival, they were completely exhausted. The villagers hid them, fed them and let them sleep. When Roberto Cofresí woke up after many hours of sleep, it was midnight of the following day. He went out alone to the Playa Marota beach where he looked for certain trees and rocks leading him to the place where he'd buried several small chests of gold coins a few weeks prior to his capture. He found them without much difficulty. The next morning Roberto gave some gold coins to his friend in the village, Ramon Leonor, in return for provisions and weapons. From another friend in this same village he bought a boat for five gold coins. The four fugitives under the command of Roberto Cofresí y Ramírez de Arellano were Ricardo González, Manuel Reyes Paz, a crew member of the pirate ship *Escipion*, the Haitian soldier Manuel Daniel, and Jaime Portalatin. When they were about to set sail, two other volunteers joined them. One of them was a young boy from Venezuela, Vicente Jimenez, and a 33-year-old man from a nearby village who went by the name of Vicente del Valle Carvajal. Both had experience as sailors.

Other historians offer a slightly different version of Cofresí 's escape from the Ozama Fort in Santo Domingo. They say that Roberto, accompanied with three fellow prisoners, managed to open the door of their cell in the middle of the night and using the a rope made from their own clothes, they descended to the Ozama River and swam away. Nevertheless, all the sources agree that he went to the region of today's Playa Marota where he bought a boat from local fishermen. It is obvious that he did not carry any money escaping from the prison; so the only possibility is that he did indeed dig up one of his treasure caches he had hidden close by.

Cofresí happily agreed, because he was in need of additional crewmembers. Wasting no time, they set sail. Shortly after they passed Saona Island, they crossed the Mona Cannel unseen, and finally landed outside of Punta Lima in Puerto Rico. Once ashore, Cofresí bluntly explained the advantages and dangers of the pirate's life to his new friends and gave them an opportunity to freely choose to stay or leave, as they liked. Portalatín, Reyes Paz and Manuel Daniel decided to stay in Puerto Rico and to start a new life. Cofresí understood, giving ten ounces of gold to each of them to help them start afresh. In return he asked them to look for some of his friends in Cabo Rojo and tell them to come and see him in three days on the island of Vieques.

Luis Asencio Camacho, an author and historian from Puerto Rico, claims that Portalatín stayed with Roberto Cofresí as a member of his crew and eventually died onboard of the Ana during Cofresí's last battle with the forces of Commander Sloat.

Roberto was certain that his former comrades would want to join him. Meanwhile he was informed that a newly constructed sailing vessel, the *Ana*, was at anchor in the small port of Fajardo. The captain of this ship was ashore and there were only two of her crew still aboard. Cofresí and three of his followers, Gonzáles, Carvajal, and Jiménez, boarded the *Ana* in the middle of the night, quickly took over control and quietly sailed off. They sailed to Punta Lima and anchored. Cofresí and Carvajal then took a skiff and rowed to Vieques where they waited for more of Cofresí 's friends to join them. Gonzales and Jimenez were left on the *Ana*. As planned, within two days several of Roberto Cofresí's confederates joined him. Antonio Delgado, Victoriano Saldaña, Juan Carlos de la Torre, Juan Manuel Fuentes and Jose Coutiño did not hesitate a moment and happily agreed to become pirates under the command of their idol, Roberto Cofresí y Ramírez de Arellano. By the end of the second night, Cofresí had assembled a contingent of 17 men in total.

Within days the newly formed gang managed to steal an appropriate vessel in Vieques, which Cofresí put to immediate use as a pirate ship. In Munacao he stole a small cannon from a ship under construction. He returned to Vieques to embark the rest of his men and set sail for the Mona Channel. Before long, Cofresí's pirate ship became the bane of all sailing masters in the Caribbean, and there were others to fear besides.

On the 9th of October of 1824 several prisoners escaped from the prison in San Juan, Puerto Rico, including Juan Manuel de Fuentes, Juan Rodríguez, and Antonio de Castillo, all of whom were former associates of Roberto Cofresí. There was also a man by the name of Bibián Hernández Morales, who joined them in the escape. He was considered an expert with a knife.

In Havana on the 19th of December of 1821, he was sentenced to 8 years in prison. In April of 1822 he arrived in Puerto Rico to serve his sentence in the prison of San Juan. Morales instantly became the leader of the escapees.

These brazen outlaws wasted no time in the resumption of their heinous trade under the command of their former leader. On the 24th of October they robbed a business in the city of Santomas and fled with at least 5,000 dollars. The next day a war ship of the United States, the *USS Beagle*, under the command of Capt. Charles Platt, left the harbor of Santomas in search of the pirates that were believed to have escaped aboard a stolen ship. This is the point in time where Bibián Hernández Morales and his gang joined Roberto Cofresí.

During the Christmas season of 1824 another group of prisoners escaped from jail and days later they joined Cofresí's band as well. Now Roberto Cofresí had more men than he needed for one ship, so he divided his men and half of them he put under the command of his right hand, Bibián Hernández Morales. They operated two armed ships and one smaller vessel.

Roberto Cofresí generally forced the crews of his victim ships to jump over the rail and swim for their lives after he'd taken everything of value. He then let his prey sail on without any control, at the will of the wind and currents. Many of these looted vessels hit the reefs or took on water and sank. Only a few of them were found before destroying themselves and delivered back to their respective owners.

In 1819 the American Congress approved 60 million dollars for the construction of five war ships, which were to be sent to the Caribbean in order to wipe out the pirates forever. These ships were the *Alligator*, the *Dolphin*, the *Shark*, the *Porpoise*, and the *Grampus*. On the 20th of December of 1822, David Porter, an American hero in the War of 1812, was named as Supreme Commander of the naval squadron in the Caribbean and the Gulf of Mexico. Porter also enjoyed a very successful record in the persecution of pirates in Algeria, Tunis, and Tripoli, aka the "Barbary Pirates".

Porter's fleet consisted of 16 war ships, and 5 small auxiliary ships. In total he had 133 cannon, and a total crew of 1,250 sailors. Porter departed on the 14th of February of 1823 from Chesapeake Bay and he arrived in the harbor of Santomas in Puerto Rico on the 12th of March. He selected this harbor as his base of operations. Later, on the 16th of November of 1824, Porter sailed off to Cuba and Haiti leaving two of his ships, the *Grampus* and the *Beagle*, to hunt down pirates in the area of Puerto Rico and the Virgin Islands. Their respective commanders were John D. Sloat and Charles T. Platt. Sloat would be the end of Cofresí.

Cofresí's small pirate fleet occasionally acted in concert. It seems, according to the testimony of his victims, that he would always appear out of nowhere and easily captured his prey. According to records, Cofresí 's band would loot two or three ships per week. In January 1825 they captured a small merchant ship, the *Neptuno*, which was sailing from the Virgin Islands to Puerto Rico. The owner/captain was Salvador Pastorisa. Under oath he declared that he could recognize Roberto Cofresí and his second in command, Pedro Salovi, among the ten assailants who robbed him of his ship and cargo. Pedro Salovi was an Italian, married to a Puerto Rican girl, who joined Cofresí in Vieques. Salovi was killed after two short months with Cofresí.

Cofresí 's pirates routinely took the cargo and money found on their captive ships, and all the jewelry and valuables of the crew and passengers, after which they would permit their victims to continue on their way. In February 1825 Cofresí captured and looted three Danish merchants of the same ship owner in the vicinity of Puerto Rico. The first two were easy prey but the crew of the third one refused to surrender and resisted. The pirates killed all seven crewmembers, and after taking everything of value, they burned the ship.

In early February 1825, an insolent squad of Cofresí's pirates, 35 men in all, attacked the US warship *USS Beagle*. While the battle raged, another US war ship appeared and they quickly finished the fight. All the pirates who survived were put in irons and sent back to jail. Bibián Hernández was among them and his loss proved to be a strong blow to Roberto Cofresí.

Cofresí managed to capture a brand new merchant ship, the *Anne*, under the command of John Low. The owner, Mr. Toribio Centeno, had taken her on her maiden voyage to the harbor of Fajardo. While the *Anne* was at anchor, Roberto Cofresí, with eight of his fellows, boarded the ship in the middle of the night, forcing Low and his crew to jump over the side to save their lives. This was the last ship used by Cofresí. He renamed her the *Ana*. It's said that Roberto took this ship as an act of vengeance against John Low, who'd helped to capture his right hand man, Bibián Hernández Morales, just a month earlier.

Early in March 1825 Roberto secretly visited his wife and daughter and left her with 2,500 ounces of gold for his brother Ignacio. By this time there were many ships sailing under the American flag and those of other Anglo nations that had been looted by Cofresí. He had become a substantial threat and the American government insisted on taking immediate action against this fearsome pirate.

The last battle of
Roberto Cofresí y Ramírez de Arellano

When John Sloat was informed of merchant ships being attacked and captured in the vicinity of Fajardo in Puerto Rico during the first days of March 1825, he did not hesitate and immediately set sail for that port. The American commander prepared an ambush for Roberto Cofresí. He disguised his ship, the *Grampus* using wood panels that hid his cannon, giving his vessel the appearance of an innocent merchantman. Of the 95 men onboard, one third were marines, hidden below deck. Another armed ship, the *Dolphin* was sailing close by to provide assistance if needed.

On the 5th of March *Ana* was stationed in the bay of Boca de Infierno. The pirate watch suddenly spied sails on the horizon and Cofresí wasted no time in giving the orders for immediate pursuit. The disguised *Grampus* pretended to escape but when the Cofresí ship was close to them and the pirates prepared to board the *Grampus*, Commander Sloat gave the order to open fire.

There are actually two slightly different versions of this battle. A Spanish version cites the Grampus under the command of John Sloat, but the American version claims that Commander Pendergrast and his ship, the Dolphin, actually captured Roberto Cofresí. Considering that Commander Sloat visited Roberto Cofresí in jail between the 18th and 19th of March, the Spanish version would seem to be the accurate report.

It was too late for the pirates to turn back at this point, but they may have entertained the idea of reversing their fortunes by out maneuvering the *Grampus*. Cofresí had six cannon, and his crew were quick to man them, however, the battle lasted for 45 minutes when a hole was opened in the hull of the *Ana* and she began to take on water. Some historians claim that Cofresí was flying the flag of Columbia during the battle, while others claim he flew the banner of Free Puerto Rico.

By now the pirates realized they had made a deadly mistake. The *Grampus* cannon coupled with the sharp shooting marines had taken their toll. Roberto Cofresí was injured and he ordered his helmsman to steer for nearby shallow waters, intending to beach his ship and escape in the numerous mangrove channels. The remaining 17 members of Cofresí's crew were in a state of confusion when a number of marines appeared behind their ship's rail and let loose another volley of musket lead. Most of the pirates then jumped into the water as the *Ana* approached the shore. *Ana* was already full of holes and was sinking. Cofresí, Carvajal and another crewmember by the name of Ricardo, tried to get out of musket range as they swam for their lives toward shore. Commander Sloat was sure that he could easily capture the escaping pirate captain and lost several valuable minutes maneuvering under sail. The pirates swam ashore where the *Grampus* could not reach them. Commander Sloat quickly realized their advantage and lowered a longboat to give chase.

Cofresí and his two confederates succeeded in concealing themselves in the mangroves as the soldiers hunted for them. Eventually they ran across the little island to the far side where the game of hide and seek continued for some time as the trio concealed themselves in mangrove debris. They began moving toward the mainland, but were noticed by a soldier in the longboat. But it was too late... Cofresí, Ricardo, and Carvajal had reached the mainland shore where they ran into the forest. Seven other pirate survivors had also managed to escape separately. One of these survivors was Juan Carlos de la Torre. None of the pirates knew that a squadron of Spanish soldiers was also looking for them on shore, thanks to the quick notification of Vicente Antoneti, who had been in the company of Commander Sloat when the battle began. Antoneti notified Spanish authorities and they, in turn, mustered troops to close the trap from the land's side of the action.

Meanwhile, American soldiers boarded the abandoned, sinking *Ana*, confiscating everything on board. Commander Sloat appointed a small crew to stay aboard *Ana* to make the necessary repairs that would keep her afloat, so that she might be returned to the harbor of Fajardo and her captain, John Low, who'd been very helpful during the expedition against Cofresí.

At some point, Juan Carlos de la Torre came upon Roberto and his two companions and he joined up with them. The foursome was then spotted by an army patrol and a fight ensued. The pirates were seriously wounded despite their fierce resistance, and Cofresí, in particular, was felled by three saber wounds that finally left him unconscious upon the ground. The fight was over. All four of them, severely injured, were taken to the village of Guayama where a local doctor by the name of Roso provided first aid to the pirates and especially to their captain.

Three days passed before Cofresí and his band could be transported to the main prison in San Juan's El Morro fortress. Upon their arrival at El Morro a special contingent of 25 soldiers was assigned to guard them, lest they make another successful escape. Records indicate that Cofresí offered a bribe of 4,000 pesos to the mayor of Guayama if he would release him from that city's jail, prior to his transfer to El Morro. That quantity of pesos weighed in at over thirty pounds of silver, at that time, but the mayor knew that repercussions from the central government were too fearsome if he permitted Cofresí to escape.

There are many historical documents that claim Roberto Cofresí was captured by Spanish soldiers under the command of Lieutenant Manuel Marcano but this is not true. A group of four local militiamen discovered Cofresí and his companions in the forest. These men were fed up with the unending assaults and continual thefts by brigands acting under the directions of Roberto Cofresí. These volunteers wanted to put an end to this dangerous gang once and for all. A local fisherman fired the shot from a short-barreled trabuco that hit Cofresí in his left arm and sent him to the ground. A single fisherman finally managed to take down Cofresí... something that the whole Spanish army in Puerto Rico could not do during the course of four long years.

Commander Sloat arrived in San Juan harbor aboard the Grampus on the 14th of March 1825 and stayed there four days. During his stay, the governor of Ponce, Don Miguel de la Torre, and Commander Tomas Renovales expressed in writing their appreciation for the help of the United States in the capture of Roberto Cofresí. Commander Sloat visited Cofresí in jail, but instead of finding a depressed and broken man, Cofresí insulted him, telling him that if he'd had more time, he would have assaulted and looted many more American ships.

Above: an illustration created during the early 20th century to
depict the capture of Cofresí with his schooner Ana, on the right

As the days passed other members of the Cofresí crew were captured by Spanish patrols. Vicente Carvajal was apprehended together with other two pirates in the town of Jobos. On the 6th of March 1825, the governor of Guayama, Francisco Brenes, notified the governor and General Captain of the island about the capture of the infamous pirate, Roberto Cofresí. Two days later, on the 8th of March, Juan Carlos Torres and Jose Miguel Fuentes were caught and the following day, others were taken prisoner.

The trial of the pirates began on March 25th. Roberto Cofresí testified about the ships he had captured and looted, about the stolen goods and money on board, but he refused to talk about the fate of certain crews and ships. The hearing lasted for two days and the final sentence was read by the judge on Sunday, the 27th of March 1825. All 11 pirates were sentenced to death by firing squad. The execution was scheduled for the 29th of March, at 8 o'clock in the morning. The last night before the execution, the eleven pirates were permitted a final wish. Four of them asked for a pardon, three wished that everybody would go to hell, three kept silent, and Roberto Cofresí asked for a pencil, paper, and privacy.

The only person given clemency was a young black servant of Roberto Cofresí by the name of Carlos, who was sold for 133 pesos as a slave to a colonel of the Spanish troops in San Juan. This money served as a partial payment for the whole trial that cost 643 pesos, 2 reales, and 12 maravedis. The rest was collected from the Mattei brothers in the harbor city of San German, who auctioned some of the stolen goods. On a side note: Carlos died a few months later.

The list of executed pirates, the crew of Roberto Cofresí:

- Roberto Cofresí y Ramírez de Arellano – 34 years old, from Puerto Rico
- Manuel Aponte (alias Monteverde) – 25 years old, from Puerto Rico
- Vicente del Valle Carvajal – 33 years old, from Hispaniola
- Vicente Jimenez – 19 years old, from Venezuela
- Antonio Delgado – 27 years old, from Puerto Rico
- Victoriano Saldaña – 28 years old, from Puerto Rico
- Agustín de Soto – 28 years old, from Puerto Rico
- Carlos Díaz – 30 years old, from Trinidad
- Carlos Torres – 22 years old, from Puerto Rico
- Juan Manuel Fuentes – 22 years old, from Cuba
- José Rodríguez – from Argentina

Early in the morning of the 29th of March, hundreds spectators began arriving to see the execution. The Spanish authorities were worried about this mob, many of them being sympathizers with the pirate, so the governor dispatched soldiers of Granada Infantry Regiment to keep order. Soldiers of this Regiment also formed part of the firing squad. The Prince of Pirates, Black Eagle of the Caribbean, and his fellow pirates were tied to poles behind the walls of fort San Felipe del Morro. Roberto Cofresí alone refused to be blinded by black ribbon before his execution, claiming that he had seen the death of at least 300 or 400 persons so he wanted to see it coming to him as well. Roberto Cofresí y Ramírez de Arellano and his 10 friends died after being shot to death by firing squad shortly after 8 o'clock in the morning. The event was announced in the official newspaper, La Gaceta, that same day.

Cofresí and his men were buried behind the cemetery, at the place where a green hill can be found today that overlooks the cemetery's original wall. They were not buried in the Old San Juan Cemetery, as was originally believed, since they were executed as criminals and therefore they could not be laid to rest in this Catholic cemetery among other Christians. But there is also a rumor that the bodies of all 11 pirates were buried in a common grave in the cemetery of Santa Magdalena de Pazzis, located outside the walls of El Morro.

To operate as effectively as he did, Cofresí needed a huge support network in Puerto Rico and Hispaniola. He had spies that advised him when certain cargos were at sea and what ships they were on. He had people that used the black market to sell his stolen booty. He had others who provided him with victuals and weapons, and there were those who kept him abreast of government ship movements. His well-organized system took fourteen years to completely dismantle.

The truth is often stranger than fiction... When the Spanish Queen discovered that Roberto Cofresí had been captured she also knew that he would be condemned to death. She immediately wrote a letter giving him a king's pardon and issued a legal corso patent to him. Her logic for this was simple: Cofresí primarily attacked foreign ships and according to Spain, each foreign ship in the Caribbean was considered to be a smuggler and was, therefore, the enemy of the Crown. Roughly 80 corsairs from Puerto Rico dedicated themselves to the destruction of foreign ships around the island, as there were few Spanish warships in the area. The principals among them included the likes of Jose Almeyda, Portuguese by origin, Manuel Lamparo, Dominican and, of course, Roberto Cofresí. Whatever the case, the queen's letter arrived at Puerto Rico two days after the execution of the entire crew of Roberto Cofresí. Many people were surprised by the queen's empathy because a few months prior to his capture, Cofresí successfully looted the Spanish merchant ship *San José y Las Animas* north of Puerto Rico. Despite the fact that this vessel was small and only had a crew of four, it was a regular transport for consumables between Cabo Rojo and the south side of the island and Cofresí's attack upon her made the Spanish authorities furious.

Cofresí himself declared that he began attacking Spanish ships when he felt that the Spaniards were oppressing the Puerto Ricans in their own country.

Upon hearing of her husband's execution, Juana Creitoff suffered a heart attack. She never fully recovered from it and died the following year on May 6th, 1826. That same month of May, but a day earlier, two more pirates were executed in the same place and in the same fashion as Roberto Cofresí – Manuel Lamparo, a Dominican, and James Leon, who was originally from Liverpool, England. The last Cofresí pirate, José de Almeyda, was caught and hanged in 1832. And with Almeyda's death, piracy in the Caribbean came to an end.

There were many Cofresí sympathizers among local inhabitants, during his life and after his death as well. There were so many that fourteen years after his death in 1839, some of them were still being put in jail! Roberto's own brothers, Ignacio and Francisco, were charged by Spanish authorities as pirate collaborators and spent two years in prison, from 1824 to 1826. The harbor captain of Cabo Rojo, don José Mendoza and the ex-governor of the city of Mayagüez, José María Ramirez de Arellano (relative of Roberto) had problems with authorities because of him. With the death of Roberto Cofresí the days of great pirate personalities in the Caribbean were over. There were still pirates, but none would be so notably successful in the Caribbean until John Boysie Singh, nicknamed "The Rajah", prowled the sea in the 20th century.

Legend says that Roberto Cofresí placed a curse on Captain Sloat and the *USS Grampus* before he died. In 1848, the *Grampus* was indeed lost at sea with all hands, however, Captain Sloat was not among the dead. Sloat eventually became the Commander of the Norfolk Navy Yard.

Roberto Cofresí becomes a pirate

One evening, Roberto gathered eight of his closest compadres together and regaled them to take their own destinies into their own hands, to carve out their own wealth from the world, and turn justice on its head. Each of these eight men swore their allegiance to Roberto, unto death. Roberto made the same proposals to his brother Ignacio, and his brother-in-law Miguel, but both of them denied his challenge, preferring a steady, quiet life on land.

From that fateful evening forward, Roberto and his motley crew began scheming to begin their criminal enterprise. First, they must have weapons, and second, they must have a vessel. Any boat suitable for a voyage to Samana would do; Roberto made inquiries of one of his relatives, a childhood friend, Joaquin Hernandez. He implored Joaquin to find a suitable craft that would serve them in their new life as pirates. Before the pair knew it, an opportunity came into view. An unattended boat was now at anchor in the harbor of Cabo Rojo where its captain and crew were ashore obtaining provisions. Roberto, Joaquin's father, Eusebio Hernández from Samaná, and brothers Juan and José Almeyda, managed to steal the boat in the middle of the night and set sail for Samaná on the neighboring island of Hispaniola. On arrival the group was joined by Joaquin's friend Campechano, along with two other men from Samana. Things were very difficult in Cabo Rojo where, for example, a small barge, Las Pascuas, waited for weeks on end to carry a small cargo to Santo Domingo. Life was hard, and money was slim.

Now that his pirate crew was assembled and ready to go, Roberto Cofresí and seven of his men decided to steal a small ship, *El Mosquete*, which was anchored nearby. *El Mosquete* suited their purposes exactly. One night they took the boat's sleeping crew by surprise and sailed to the bottom of the bay where they tied the captain and the three crewmen to a tree. The incident left none of the parties of either side injured. Cofresí had maneuvered *El Mosquete* through channels between the mangroves, a risky business, but one in which he was particularly adept... he knew the area like the back of his hand. He managed to have his companions tow the boat through the channels to a small lake about two kilometers (approximately 1.25 miles) inland, where they careened the vessel, painted her hull black and removed her title boards, replacing them with new ones that now read "*El Mosquito*". It took them three days to make these cosmetic changes to their new pirate ship. Since *El Mosquete* was ready to sail when she was stolen, there were sufficient stores aboard to maintain Cofresí and his gang.

Again, there are historians that say that his first pirate ship was called Relámpago, which means "Lightning" in English, in honor of his first small boat that was purposefully rammed and destroyed by an English merchant ship in the bay of Cabo Rojo.

Meanwhile, the dispossessed crew of *El Mosquete*, finally freed by some local fishermen, had begun to search for their missing ship throughout the region of Samana Peninsula, Cabrera, and as far west as Puerto Plata along the northern coast of present-day Dominican Republic. They continued to hunt for their "white" ship, not knowing that it had been painted black by the Cofresí gang. Nobody considered that Cofresí had actually hidden deep behind the mangroves, a scheme that seemed to be stupid, if not impossible. However, this was the genius of Roberto Cofresí, and a talent that served him well over the span of his criminal career... he did the thing that was unexpected. As mentioned, after three days the *El Mosquito* was ready to sail, painted black, with a stolen tender tied to her stern. She sneaked through the bay during hours of darkness and made her way toward Bahia Escocesa (Scottish Bay), also known as Bahia Colberg, on the lookout for the first victims.

Before long their first merchant ship victim appeared. It was a small barge and the four men crew did not offer any resistance when Cofresí boarded them. He'd left *El Mosquito* with the seventy-year-old Hernandez Senior and his son, Joaquin, who was twenty. According to narrations of the descendents of Joaquin Hernandez, when Cofresí took over this prize, he interrogated the captain and discovered that the vessel was underway from Montecristi to Santo Domingo with ten sacks of rice, salted fish and a single passenger, Luis Delarus. It seems that the passenger was well off, and the pirates relieved him of a small chest of gold coins, hidden in the rope locker. After stripping the vessel of her cargo, she was sent on her way and the rice and fish was transferred to the *El Mosquito*. Cofresí's band then made their way to the vicinity of Samana where they approached land in a skiff after dark. The pirates visited with their respective families, left them some of the gold and some of the rice and buried the remainder of the gold coins nearby. The band determined this was a good idea as a form of insurance. Roberto buried the trove after rowing into the bottom of the bay during the following night. This cache was allegedly buried on a small cay known as Pancho Macho.

The following morning *El Mosquito* set sail for Cabo Rojo. Roberto took some of the captured provisions to his wife, spent a day with her and their daughter and then departed for new adventures. A rough sea caused some damage to *El Mosquito* that required immediate attention, so Roberto sailed to the small fishing village of Sol, close to the town of San Pedro de Macoris on the southern coast of Hispaniola where he knew a very good carpenter, Ramon Leonor. After four days the ship was repaired and Cofresí set sail once more.

While sailing leisurely toward Mona Island Cofresí intercepted a merchant ship whose crew refused to surrender and a fiery battle ensued wherein deaths occurred on both vessels. Roberto Cofresí almost lost his life in this battle but in the end the pirate crew was victorious. The pirates left the victim crew on a desolate island but they took the young daughter of the captain they'd slain with them. The booty was considerable. They divided it amongst themselves and sailed back to Samaná, where they stayed a couple of days anchored in front of Anandel Beach. Roberto gave part of the booty to his relatives, the Hernández family in Samaná.

Cain, one of the pirates in the Cofresí crew, was unhappy with the division of the booty and he tried to murder Cofresí one night as he slept in his cabin on board of *El Mosquito* while the boat was still anchored in Samaná. The previously mentioned young girl woke up at the last moment to warn Roberto and he managed to kill his assassin with a pistol shot. Cofresí later delivered the girl to his friend, Father José Antonio Pieretti, a priest who lived in the small village of Yauco in Puerto Rico. Cofresí also gave him a considerable amount of money to assist in the return of the girl to her family.

Roberto decided that it was in his own interest to hide the remainder of his booty somewhere other than the cabin of his ship! He enlisted the help of Joaquin Hernandez, and in the dead of night, rowed to the lower coastline of Samana Bay. The pair carried a heavy chest to a small cay where they buried it, and marked the spot with a rock. With the deed done, they rowed back to *El Mosquito*, and along the way, Roberto instructed Joaquin to provide Roberto's family with the treasure in the event of his death.

Above: the harbor of Santa Barbara de Samaná today. The bottom of the bay can be seen in the distance.

The pirates remained at anchor for several days in front of Playa Anadel (Anadel beach), near the town of Santa Barbara de Samaná. Joaquín Hernánez and Roberto Cofresí spent this time planning their next move, plotting the area where they might search for their prey. Meanwhile the remaining crew maintained guard aboard *El*

Mosquito. It's said that Rosa Hernandez, Joaquín Hernández's younger sister, successfully seduced Roberto and they had a short romantic interlude on Anadel beach.

The days quickly passed and now it was late summer of 1823. Cofresí and his crew were waiting in ambush for their next victim in the vicinity of Cape Haitien, close to Fort Liberté where the harbor of Bayaya had prospered centuries earlier. At last they spied sails on the horizon. Wasting no time, they took up pursuit and after a couple of hours they boarded their victim. She was a French merchant sailing vessel, the *Burdeos*. The ship was fairly new and lighter than *El Mosquito* so Roberto decided to take this boat as his own. He abandoned *El Mosquito* near shore along with the crew of the *Burdeos* and set sail. He changed the name of this new pirate ship to *Black Eagle*. Then they sailed to the small village of Estero Balsa, close to today's Manzanillo on the northern coast of the Dominican Republic, where they cast off part of the stolen cargo that was not of any use, especially the heavy iron anchor chain, leaving it on the beach. This long heavy chain, abandoned on the beach, was the source of a legend, the infamous "chain of Cofresí." The legend claims that whoever finds the end of the chain may follow it into the sea where they will discover a chest full of treasure.

The *Black Eagle* remained at anchor for several days before the beach of a small fishing village, Puerto Juanita, close to today's Punta Rusia. This was a favorite retreat of our pirate and he retired there after almost all of his exploits to relax, share booty with the locals, enjoy some time with his local girlfriend, Gisela Lamparo. She was an 18-year-old beauty who fell in love with the handsome and courageous pirate who allegedly had a son by him. As recently as 1987, local fishermen referred to the rock in the bay where Cofresí used to tie up his ship as "Piedra de Cofresí" (Rock of Cofresí).

Roberto Cofresí now decided to try his luck in a different location, so he sailed in the direction of Mona Passage, hoping to catch some merchant ships sailing from Santo Domingo to the harbors of Cabo Rojo or Mayagüez in Puerto Rico. Just a few days after crossing the waters near Mona Island, Cofresí spotted a small cargo ship. It was the 86-ton *John*, under the command of Daniel Knight flying the American flag. The pirates went in pursuit and finally they overcame merchant ship near Isla de Desecheo. This was toward the end of October 1823. The pirate's booty turned out to be tobacco and provisions valued at about 1,000 dollars. They also stole the spare sails. Cofresí's gang then left the *John* under control of her crew and sailed away. Captain Knight entered the harbor of Mayagüez on the 30th of October and immediately reported the incident to the governor of the city.

On the 27th of November of 1823, Roberto Cofresí and his band captured and looted a much larger American merchant ship, the *William Henry*, of 166 tons, owned by William Grey. The already furious governor of Mayaguez asked U.S. authorities for help and they sent an armed ship with the intention of eliminating the pirates, especially Roberto Cofresí. The ship sent by the U.S. to hunt down the pirates was commanded by Capt. Labonisse and the mission ended with certain success, when they found a pirate base on Saona Island along the southern coast of Hispaniola. Labonisse captured 18 pirates, and recovered a considerable amount of merchandise, tobacco, hides and money. All this recovered property, together with the pirates in irons, were taken back to New York in January, 1824. Unfortunately, none of these pirates were part of the Cofresí crew.

Mona Channel was, at the time, heavily infested with pirates. Several nations felt themselves threatened by these pirates and subsequently dispatched armed ships to remove them. The Republic of Gran Colombia sent two corvettes, the *Bocayá* and the *Bolivar*, with the specific mission of re-taking the Colombian ship *Orinoco* whose crew had mutinied and taken control of *Orinoco* by force. Following the mutiny, the *Orinoco* had assaulted merchants sailing in the Mona Channel.

Roberto Cofresí's victim tally increased quickly, and it is said that the brave captain often went to on shore in the middle of the night to bury his part of the treasure. There were no banks at the time nor other institutions where he could deposit looted gold and silver. He evidently preferred the policy of burying his fortune in various portions at different places around the island to cover any urgent needs in the future. Legend has it that he buried some treasure chests in the vicinity of the port of Maimon, at the extreme tip of Diamante Beach, close to Cabrera on the northern coast of Hispaniola, and also around Cabo Frances Viejo (Old French Cape), also on the northern coast of Hispaniola. It is also said that he buried at least two chests with gold and silver coins, and with jewelry around the beach of Puerto Juanita. Roberto Cofresí was an extremely successful pirate thanks to his courage, dedication, and intelligence... and because his entire crew, regardless of any danger, followed him blindly.

There is one incident, confirmed by numerous historians, regarding a pursuit of Cofresí's ship by Spanish authorities into Samana Bay where Cofresí abandoned his ship and he and his crew escaped into the mangroves in a longboat where the Spaniards could not follow. This occurred at Punta Gorda, close to a town known today as Sanchez, previously better known as Las Canitas. The story claims that Cofresí abandoned his loot as well. I'm told that there have been several attempts to locate the abandoned pirate ship to no avail. Unfortunately, no one seems to know the exact name of the ship in question, as the issue of ship names pedigreed to Cofresí's brigands is a cloudy one, indeed. Cofresí renamed his vessels frequently, a practice that makes serious research difficult.

In the fall of 1823, Roberto established a small operations base on Mona Island. However when he attacked the previously mentioned *William Henry*, he overtaxed the patience of the American government and they sent a squadron of two small warships to find him. The *U.S.S. Spark*, under the command of John T. Newton, and the *U.S.S. Weasel* set upon Mona Island and destroyed Cofresí's base in February of 1824; but the pirates managed to escape in time. The Americans were not the only ones searching for Roberto Cofresí and his band of pirates. In February of 1824 the República de Colombia dispatched their ship, *General Bolivar*, to round up the fearsome pirate from Puerto Rico. In a peculiar twist of fate, the skipper of the *General Bolivar* was none other than Renato Beluche, who'd once served under the infamous Jean Laffite. Beluche was not completely successful: he did manage to rescue the crews of the English merchant *Boniton* and the French merchant ship, *Bonne Sophie*... this expedition was later well documented in the Colombian press.

After losing his base of operations on Mona Island, Roberto received news that his brother Ignacio had married the daughter of a rich merchant from Cabo Rojo. Her name was María Monserrate.

Roberto wanted to be a part of the wedding of his beloved brother but he knew that it would be suicide. The Spanish garrisons from Montecristi to Samaná were on the lookout for him following several months of intrepid and very successful pirate expeditions.

The Black Eagle was of intense interest to Spanish authorities all along the entire northern coast of Hispaniola.

Before sailing south, Roberto decided to hide a chest full of gold and his chosen hiding spot was the mouth of the Yuma River close to Samaná Bay. At low tide he buried his chest under the exposed sandy bottom of the river. He knew that high tide would cover the spot with water and his treasure would be more than safe there.

Roberto Cofresí then spent several months marauding along the southern coast of the island. He anchored for a short time in the Higuano river mouth close to the town of San Pedro Macoris. Then he went to Los Almendros Beach a few kilometers south of the city of Baní, where he captured two merchant ships. He supposedly buried another of his treasures in the vicinity of this beach as well. Sailing west he stopped at the mouth of the Neiba River, close to the city of Barahona where the pirates went ashore. They waited there for new victims without success, so Cofresí decided to move westward, to one of his favorite places, in the shadow of the Beata Island and its rocky neighboring island, Alto Velo. Days passed without sighting a new victim.

The impatient pirate captain then decided to sail back to the north shore of Hispaniola where the maritime traffic was considerably heavier, but also much more dangerous for the likes of himself and his crew of desperados. They arrived at one of their favorite ambush points on the northern coast, El Diamante Beach.

Note: El Diamante Beach was destroyed by an earthquake and tsunami in 1946.

A day after dropping anchor here, the pirates captured, boarded, and ransacked a Spanish merchant vessel, the *Celeste*. Cofresí decided to sail to Puerto Juanita, towing the captured ship behind him. Roberto wanted to spend some days with his girlfriend and share some of the booty with the locals as was his usual custom. While entering the anchorage, the pirate ship *Black Eagle* suddenly capsized and sank. Everybody on board was saved, but all cargo went to the bottom. So the pirates now had to use the *Celeste* as their new ship. Roberto christened her the *Ana*.

After relaxing for a few days Cofresí sailed to the small fishing village of Sabana del Mar. Roberto Cofresí frequented a nearby cave along the shore, which is still known as "Cofresí Cave". It's said that the pirate captain had a romantic encounter here with a local girl, Pilar Hernández, who fell completely in love with him, claiming she would follow him to the gates of Hell.

At this time a new governor of Puerto Rico came on the scene and one of his main goals was to cleanse the island of pirates, with Roberto Cofresí being of particular interest. The new governor, Miguel del la Torre, was aware of Cofresí's rumored support infrastructure on Puerto Rico, manifested through his connection to the powerful family of Ramirez de Arellano. Believing that the Arellano family was responsible for the distribution and marketing of Roberto Cofresí's ill-gotten goods, as well as playing a principal role in abetting his customary escape, the governor made an issue of degrading the Arellano family's influence in Puerto Rico. The governor went so far as to jail some of Roberto's relatives, charging them with conspiracy against the Spanish Crown. De la Torre was keenly aware that the United States was close to making war on Puerto Rico because of the many acts of piracy the U.S. had endured in Puerto Rican waters.

In March 1824 the French joined with the Americans and sent some of their own naval forces to capture this pirate as well, in answer to his attacks on French merchants. According to the Puerto Rican historian, Walter Cardona Bonet, Cofresí was in command of a small fleet of pirate ships during this period. Roberto was captain of his flagship *Ana*, while his second in command, Bibián Hernández Morales, was in charge of small squad of attack boats. The crews of these small pirate boats were easily recruited from prison escapees who'd fled captivity in San Juan during 1824.

During one incident, Roberto Cofresí captured an American merchant and the booty was a rich cargo valued in many dollars. He left seven members of the crew unharmed, tied up on La Parguera

Beach, where they were found some days later. It was now the beginning of March 1824. According to another historian from Puerto Rico, Aurelio Tio, Cofresí captured an American merchant sailing vessel on the 29th of May 1824, taking $8,000 from their crew. He took this ship with him to the island of Matel, but when he noticed that the Spanish were giving chase, he burnt his prize and sailed for Mona Island, one of his favorite hideouts. Roberto Cofresí, now annointed by the Spaniards as the "Terror of the Seas", was a wanted man with a reward for his capture, dead or alive. They even sent a professional mercenary by the name of Solís, disguised as a poor sailor looking for job, to kill him. But spies warned Roberto in time and in a duel on the beach Cofresí killed Solis, slicing his throat with his dagger.

On the 9th of June 1824, Roberto Cofresí and his pirate crew spotted a merchant ship in a distance. It was the *San Jose y Las Animas*, a small Spanish ship of 27 tons transporting goods between different harbors on the southern coast of Puerto Rico and the island of Santomas. The owner was Santos Lucca, from Yuca, and the ship was under the command of Captain Francisco Ocasio. Four other sailors served on board as crew. The ship carried cotton, tobacco and coffee, apart from other goods. Cofresí finally overtook the ship along the coast of Tallaboa. The crew, fearing for their lives, jumped overboard and swam to the nearby shore, leaving their ship and cargo to the mercy of the pirates. The cargo was valued at more than 6,000 pesos. Cofresí and his men took everything they could and sailed away. Later, part of the cargo was recovered in Cabo Rojo and delivered back to the original owners.

After disposing of the loot from *San Jose y Las Animas* by handing it over to friends on land for further sale, Roberto sailed to Mona Island to recuperate and form a new strategy. One of the members of his crew at that time was also an experienced Portuguese pirate by the name of Amaro Almeyda.

Note: there are different opinions about the real identity of the "Portuguese" among historians. Nevertheless all of them agree that he was a member of Cofresí's crew.

He was cruel man who joined Cofresí after losing his own ship *El Rayo* (The *Lightning*). He knew Mona Island very well, and he was said to have killed three women there that he captured during one of his acts of piracy. He raped them one by one and then he murdered them and buried them on the beach. The crewmembers from his ship then called this beach "Playa de Mujeres" (The Beach of Women). Almeyda was originally a well-to-do young man studying law at the university in Coimbra where he was born, but after some sort of dispute with one of his teachers he was obliged to leave his studies and so he started his life of adventure on the high seas.

While Cofresí's ship lay at anchor close to shore, most of the eleven man crew lounged about on Mona Island, slung in hammocks under the shade of the palms, while part of the crew remained aboard ship as guards during six hour shifts. They were unaware that they had been discovered by a fisherman from Puerto Rico who'd alerted authorities at Mayaguez. The governor of Mayaguez instantly sent a trio of ships to capture the pirates, especially Roberto Cofresí. Their attack was so sudden that the watch aboard Roberto's ship could do little else but jump ship and swim for shore.

The well-armed Spanish soldiers landed on the beach where Almeyda encountered them with saber and musket. He was not a match for the hoard of assailants who shot him and cut off his head. Cofresí's old friend, José (Pepe) Cartagena, whom he'd known since childhood also fell dead from several musket shots. Two other pirates were injured and laid on the beach while others were captured. The rest of the crew, four in all, seeing no real possibility to withstand the attack, preferred to escape. The attackers were afraid to follow them into the rocky terrain and they gave up the chase, returning to Mayagüez with the pirate ship and head of Almeyda. Before they left, they killed the injured pirates on the beach. During the night, Cofresí and the other survivors went to the small beach of Los Uveros where they'd hidden a boat and under cover of darkness they sailed away with the intention of reaching the coast somewhere near Santo Domingo.

Roberto Cofresí, Ricardo Gonzáles, Joaquín Hernández, and Miguel Creitoff, Roberto's brother-in-law, were now at sea, depressed and fearful ot the immediate future. But they all trusted in their clever captain, his judgment and good luck. It was now the 9th of September of 1824. The weather suddenly worsened, pitching wind and high waves arrived without warning and Cofresí tried to reach a beach somewhere around the cape of Cabo Engaño on the eastern coast of Hispaniola lest they be swallowed by the angry ocean. The tempest grew in its fury and the small boat containing the drenched pirates was thrown about in the waves like a small toy. But good luck turned its face to Roberto Cofresí once more. Within hours, the ocean threw the fragile, half-swamped boat onto the shore, near the small village of El Jovero (today this is near the town of Miches, on the south side of Samaná bay). The four pirates fell into a deep sleep without regard for the danger they now faced, as the coast was now full of Spanish soldiers looking for them. It was not long before they were found. As they enjoyed a morning meal of fruit they found growing in the area, they were quietly surrounded by a group of soldiers. They had no chance to flee. Just two days after their miraculous escape from Mona Island, Roberto Cofresí and his three friends were captured and imprisoned in the local jail.

The following day the French frigate *Fortuna* arrived to pick up Cofresí and his confederates. The *Fortuna* had been patrolling the area on the lookout for pirates, generally, and Cofresí's band in particular. Eight heavily armed men took custody of the four and took them aboard. Cofresí was left shackled, but the other three were not, and as the *Fortuna* left for Santo Domingo where the pirates would be tried, upon clearing Samana Bay, both Miguel Creitoff and Joaquín Hernández jumped overboard into the ocean. Both men were competent swimmers and at this moment they were swimming for their lives! They stroked their way toward the shallows of the shore where the *Fortuna* could not follow. Just as the pair believed they were out of danger a black fin broached the surface giving them chase. Within seconds a huge shark attacked Miguel Creitoff as parties aboard the *Fortuna* watched in horror. The ocean filled with blood.

Joaquín Hernández managed to reach the shallows and hide himself in the mangroves. Authorities aboard *Fortuna* decided this was not the time to pursue Hernandez as the most important pirate, Roberto Cofresí y Ramírez de Arellano, the "Terror of the Seas", the "Black Prince of the Caribbean", was in still in chains onboard.

Hernandez escaped, so *La Fortuna* turned her bow toward Santo Domingo and hoisted sail once more, still carrying her most wanted prisoner.

Walter Cardona states in his book that Joaquín Hernández did not jump over the rail of the French ship but that he was in the prison of Ozama Fortress with Roberto Cofresí. According to Cardona, Hernandez refused to escape from jail with his friend Roberto, instead serving a sentence of six years, after which he returned to Samaná. This is not possible. There are archived documents regarding the city of Sanchez, where it is clearly written that Joaquín Hernández, former comrade of Roberto Cofresí, founded this city in 1824. Hernandez was not aboard Roberto's ship when Roberto was caught. Hernandez was living in Samaná at the time.

Genealogy of the Cofresí family

Name: Cristoforo KUPFERSCHEIN
Given Name: Cristoforo
Surname: Kupferschein
Sex: M
Note: He is the first known ancestor of the Kupferscheim family, born in 14?? in Bohemia, (actually the Czech Republic) during the reign of Ferdinand I, King of Bohemia and Hungary, later Emperor of the Holy Roman Empire. Ferdinand I awarded Cristoforo a coat of arms with a crest and a diploma that was signed on the 3rd of December of 1549 in Prague, the capital of the Czech Republic. From Bohemia, Cristoforo went to Kaernten, Austria where he later died. His sons went first to the city of Krain in the former Yugoslavia and then finally to Trieste, Italy.
Birth: in Bohemia, Czechoslovakia
Death: in Kaerntern, Austria, in 15??
Marriage 1 Spouse Unknown

Married: in Kaerntern, Austria
Children
Fenicio VON KUPFERSCHEIN b: born in Kaerntern, Austria

===

Name: Fenicio VON KUPFERSCHEIN
Given Name: Fenicio
Surname: von Kupferschein
Sex: M
Note: The second known ancestor of the Kupferscheims. He was born in Kaernten, Austria. He was the first member of the Kupferschein family that moved to Trieste, where he was a notary in the tax office from 1588 to 1592. He was the Imperial Tax Collector in Trieste from 1602 to 1613. King Ferdinand II awarded him the diploma of Equestrian Nobility of the Holy Roman Empire and all his heirs state that was signed in Vienna, Austria on 2 April 1620. This diploma makes reference to the previous one awarded to Cristoforo by King Ferdinand I, in December 1549, and amplified the family coat-of-arms, simultaneously promoting Fenicio and all his descendants to the rank of Knights of the Holy Roman Empire. Fenicio received a Doctorate of Law degree from the University of Bologne on 23 December 1627. He is buried in the church of the Reverend Conventual's Fathers, known as San Juan Bautista, in Schwarzenegg, Austria. He had ordered a mausoleum built in the center of the church with an epitaph written by him and with his coat of arms engraved on it.

Birth: in Kaerntern, Austria
Death: on the 31st of July of 1629 in Trieste, Italy
Father: Cristoforo KUPFERSCHEIN
Marriage with Nicoletta INRICO, born on the 28th of October of 1571 in Trieste, Italy
Married: 1597 in Trieste, Italy
Children:

Gisseppe VON KUPFERSCHEIN, born in Trieste, Italy
Francesco VON KUPFERSCHEIN INRICO, born in 1602 in
Trieste, Italy

===

Name: Francesco VON KUPFERSCHEIN INRICO
Given Name: Francesco
Surname: von Kupferschein Inrico
Sex: M
Note: Fenicio's third son. He was a tax collector in Zaule. He had
three sons and four daughters.

Birth: 1602 in Trieste, Italy
Death: 1655 in Trieste, Italy

Father: Fenicio VON KUPFERSCHEIN, born in Kaerntern,
Austria
Mother: Nicoletta INRICO, born on the 28th of October of 1571
in Trieste, Italy

Married with Orsola DE VISCOVICH DE MARENZI
Day of marriage: on the 23rd of February of 1628 in Trieste, Italy
Children:
Giuseppe VON KUPFERSCHEIN DE VISCOVICH, born in
Trieste, Italy
Giovanni Antonio VON KUPFERSCHEIN DE VISCOVICH,
born on the 17th of January of 1633 in Trieste, Italy

===

Name: Giovanni Antonio VON KUPFERSCHEIN DE
VISCOVICH

Given Name: Giovanni Antonio
Surname: von Kupferschein de Viscovich
Sex: M

Note: He was admitted to the Patrician Council in 1669 and he was a state tax collector in Funfenburg, Austria. He and his wife Margarita had six sons and two daughters.

Birth: on the 17th of January of 1633 in Trieste, Italy
Baptism: on the 17th of January of 1633 in Trieste, Italy
Death: on the 20th of February of 1700 in Trieste, Italy
Burial: in February 1700 in the Church of San Francisco, Trieste, Italy

Father: Francesco VON KUPFERSCHEIN INRICO, born in 1602 in Trieste, Italy
Mother: Orsola DE VISCOVICH DE MARENZI

Marriage with Margarita Giulia BOTTONI NAUSER, who was born in April 1645 in Trieste, Italy
Married: on the 21st of June of 1666 in Trieste, Italy
Children:
Francesco Giovanni VON KUPFERSCHEIN BOTTONI, born on the 1st of February of 1671 in Trieste, Italy

===

Name: Francesco Giovanni VON KUPFERSCHEIN BOTTONI
Given Name: Francesco Giovanni
Surname: von Kupferschein Bottoni
Sex: M

Note: He was elected patrician in 1691, from 1700-1701 he was warden of the jail in Funfenburg, Austria, and from 1708 to 1722 he was a tax collector in Trieste. He had one son, Giuseppe Stanislao.

Birth: on the 1st of February of 1671 in Trieste, Italy
Death: on the 3rd of March of 1736 in Trieste, Italy

Father: Giovanni Antonio VON KUPFERSCHEIN DE VISCOVICH, born on the 17th of January of 1633 in Trieste, Italy

Mother: Margarita Giulia BOTTONI NAUSER, born in April 1645 in Trieste, Italy

Marriage with Cattarina Elena Benedetta CONTI, born on the 1st of October of 1705 in Trieste, Italy
Married: on the 4th of October of 1724 in Trieste, Italy

Children:
Giovanni Giuseppe Stanislao VON KUPFERSCHEIN CONTI, born on the 19th of November of 1725 in Trieste, Italy

==

Name: Giovanni Giuseppe Stanislao VON KUPFERSCHEIN CONTI
Given Name: Giovanni Giuseppe Stanislao
Surname: von Kupferschein Conti
Sex: M

Note: Giovanni Giuseppe and Cattarina's only son. He was admitted to the Patrician Council of Trieste on the 2nd of September of 1748. From 1762 to 1766 he held the civic position of Provident in Trieste and from 1768 to 1770 he was a judge in Trieste. On the 24th of April of 1759 he was appointed as Captain and Commander of the militia in this city and on the 3rd of October of 1770 he was also appointed as Treasurer and Counsel of the city hall of Trieste and he held these positions until his retirement for health reasons in 1787.

Birth: on the 19th of November of 1725 in Trieste, Italy

Death: on the 3rd of January of 1789 in Trieste, Italy

Residence: Via Riborgo (Via Teatro Romano) #51, Trieste, Italy from 1744 to 1752

Father: Francesco Giovanni VON KUPFERSCHEIN BOTTONI, born on the 1st of February of 1671 in Trieste, Italy

Mother: Cattarina Elena Benedetta CONTI, born on the 1st of October of 1705 in Trieste, Italy

First marriage with Maria Ana Cattarina DE FRANCOL NICOLETTI, born on the 13th of April of 1726 in Trieste, Italy

Married: on the 28th of September of 1747 in Trieste, Italy

Children:

Cattarina Maria Gioseffa VON KUPFERSCHEIN DE FRANCOL, born in 1748 in Trieste, Italy

Maria Anna Gioseffa VON KUPFERSCHEIN DE FRANCOL, born in 1749 in Trieste, Italy

Francesco Giuseppe Fortunato VON KUPFERSCHEIN (COFRESÍ), born on the 12th of July of 1751 in Trieste, Italy

Margarita Gioseffa VON KUPFERSCHEIN DE FRANCOL, born on the 7th of October of 1752 in Trieste, Italy

Second marriage with Chiara Maria SAVERTIGLIA DE RAAB, born in Trieste, Italy

Married: on March 1753 in Trieste, Italy

Children:
Giovanni VON KUPFERSCHEIM SAVERTIGLIA
Gioseffa Orsola VON KUPFERSCHEIM SAVERTIGLIA

===

Name: Francesco Giuseppe Fortunato VON KUPFERSCHEIN (COFRESÍ)
Given Name: Francesco Giuseppe Fortunato
Surname: von Kupferschein (Cofresí)
Sex: M

Note: Francesco (Franz) Giuseppe, the only son of Giovanni Giuseppe and Maria Anna Cattarina was born during the reign of Maria Teresa of Habsburg, Empress of Austria and Queen of Hungary and Bohemia. Franz went to Frankfurt, Germany when he was 19 years old and remained there until the next year. Franz returned to Trieste on February 4, 1771 and seven years later, on the 1st day of August, he left Trieste in a hurry, accused of murdering his friend Josephus Stephani.

Franz must have arrived in Cabo Rojo with considerable funds, because he bought land there. His manner and fluency in various languages must have helped him to establish social relations with the most distinguished families of the European ancestry. He met Clemente Ramirez de Arellano, first cousin of the founder of Cabo Rojo, his wife Doña Maria Concepcion Segarra and their daughter, Maria Germana whom Franz married in 1784 when he was 33 years old and she was 19. In Puerto Rico, because of the difficulty of its pronunciation, the surname suffered many changes: Kupfersein, Kufresin, Cofersin, Confercin, and finally Cofresí .

Birth: on the 12th of July of 1751 in Trieste, Italy
Death: on the 29th of September of 1814 in Cabo Rojo, Puerto Rico

Father: Giovanni Giuseppe Stanislao VON KUPFERSCHEIN CONTI, born on the 19th of November of 1725 in Trieste, Italy

Mother: Maria Ana Cattarina DE FRANCOL NICOLETTI, born on the 13th of April of 1726 in Trieste, Italy

Married in 1784 with Maria Germana RAMIREZ DE ARELLANO SEGARRA, born in 1765 in Cabo Rojo, Puerto Rico

Children:

Juana COFRESÍ RAMIREZ DE ARELLANO, born on the 21st of June of 1785 in Cabo Rojo, Puerto Rico

Juan Francisco COFRESÍ RAMIREZ DE ARELLANO, born on the 25th of March of 1787 in Cabo Rojo, Puerto Rico

Ignacio COFRESÍ RAMIREZ DE ARELLANO, born on the 27th of August of 1789 in Cabo Rojo, Puerto Rico

Roberto COFRESÍ RAMIREZ DE ARELLANO, born on the 12th of June of 1791 in El Tujao, Cabo Rojo, Puerto Rico

==

Name: Juan Francisco COFRESÍ RAMIREZ DE ARELLANO
Given Name: Juan Francisco
Surname: Cofresí Ramirez de Arellano
Sex: M

Note: Juan, the oldest son of Franz and Maria Germana, was a businessman and co-owner together with Luis del Rio (the father of Maria Monserrate del Rio Carbonell, Ignacio's wife), of the ship Monserrate. Juan married Juana Balines, daughter of Juan Balines (Balini), and Maria Sanabria.

Birth: on the 25th of March of 1787 in Cabo Rojo, Puerto Rico
Death: in Humacao, Puerto Rico

Father: Francesco Giuseppe Fortunato VON KUPFERSCHEIN (COFRESÍ), born on the 12th of July of 1751 in Trieste, Italy

Mother: Maria Germana RAMIREZ DE ARELLANO SEGARRA, born in 1765 in Cabo Rojo, Puerto Rico
Marriage with Juana VALINES SANABRIA, born in Cabo Rojo, Puerto Rico

Married: on the 25th of May of 1809 in Cabo Rojo, Puerto Rico

Children:
Juan COFRESÍ VALINES, born in 1824 in Cabo Rojo, Puerto Rico
Juana Maria COFRESÍ VALINES, born in Cabo Rojo, Puerto Rico
Maria de la Cruz COFRESÍ VALINES, born in Cabo Rojo, Puerto Rico
Maria Magdalena COFRESÍ VALINES, born in Cabo Rojo, Puerto Rico
Maria Ramona COFRESÍ VALINES, born in Cabo Rojo, Puerto Rico
Juana Josefa COFRESÍ VALINES, born on the 17th of May of 1827 in Cabo Rojo, Puerto Rico
Josefa COFRESÍ VALINES, born in Cabo Rojo, Puerto Rico
Irenes COFRESÍ VALINES, born in 1831 in Cabo Rojo, Puerto Rico
Nicolas COFRESÍ VALINES, born in Cabo Rojo, Puerto Rico
Jose Justo COFRESÍ VALINES, born in Cabo Rojo, Puerto Rico
Monserrate Gumersindo COFRESÍ VALINES, born in 1833 in Cabo Rojo, Puerto Rico
Maria Ramona COFRESÍ VALINES, born ? in ?, Puerto Rico
Ramon Cofresí VALINES, born ? in ?, Puerto Rico

==

Name: Ramon Cofresí Valines
Given Name: Ramon
Surname: Cofresí Valines
Sex: M

Father: Juan Francisco COFRESÍ RAMIREZ DE ARELLANO
Mother: Juana Balines Valines (Balines) Sanabria

Married with Manuela Herrera

Children:
Jose Miguel Cofresí, born in 1854 in Puerto Rico

===

Name: Jose Miguel Cofresí Herrera
Given Name: Jose Miguel
Surname: Cofresí Herrera
Sex: M

Father: Ramon Cofresí Valines
Mother: Manuela Herrera

Married with Paula Ayala, born in 1856

Children:
Miguel Cofresí, born in 1896 in Puerto Rico
Maria Cofresí, born in 1881 in Puerto Rico
Euclides Cofresí, born in 1890 in Puerto Rico
Domingo Cofresí, born in 1896 in Puerto Rico
Sinforiano Cofresí, born in 1878 in Puerto Rico

===

Name: Miguel Cofresí Ayala Given Name: Miguel
Surname: Cofresí Ayala
Birth: in 1896
Sex: M

Father: Jose Miguel Cofresí Herrera
Mother: Paubla Ayala Leon

Marriage with Brigida Vega, born in1897 in Patillas, Puerto Rico

Children:
Gilberto Cofresí, born on Jan 5th, 1921 in Patillas, Puerto Rico
Jose Joaquin Cofresí, born on April 4th, 1918 in Patillas, Puerto Rico
Luz Maria Cofresí, born on April 12th, 1923 in Arroyo, Puerto Rico

===

Name: Maria Cofresí Ayala
Given Name: Maria
Surname: Cofresí Ayala
Birth: in 1923
Sex: F

Father: Jose Miguel Cofresí Herrera
Mother: Paubla Ayala Leon
Married with Pablo Perez, born in 1880 (approximate) in Puerto Rico
Children: NONE

===

Name: Euclides Cofresí Ayala
Given Name: Euclides
Surname: Cofresí Ayala
Birth: in 1890
Sex: M

Father: Jose Miguel Cofresí Herrera
Mother: Paubla Ayala Leon

Married with Luisa Martinez, born in 1891 in Puerto Rico

Children:
Luis Cofresí, born in 1915 in Puerto Rico
Bernardina Cofresí, born in 1916 in Puerto Rico
Maria Monserrate Cofresí, born in 1919 in Puerto Rico
Miguel A. Cofresí, born in 1925 in Puerto Rico
Jesus M. Cofresí, born in 1922 in Puerto Rico
Juan Cofresí, born in 1927 in Puerto Rico

===

Name: Domingo Cofresí Ayala
Given Name: Domingo
Surname: Cofresí Ayala
Birth: 1896
Sex: M

Father: Jose Miguel Cofresí Herrera
Mother: Paubla Ayala Leon
Marriage with Agueda Diaz

Children:
Maria Carlota Cofresí, born in 1919 in Puerto Rico

==

Name: Sinforiano Cofresí Ayala
Given Name: Sinforiano
Surname: Cofresí Ayala
Birth: in 1881
Sex: M

Father: Jose Miguel Cofresí Herrera
Mother: Paubla Ayala Leon
Marriage with Ambrosia Cruz, born in 1888 in Puerto Rico

Children:
Antonio Cofresí, born in 1911 in Puerto Rico
Carlota Cofresí, born in 1908 in Puerto Rico
Felicita Cofresí, born in 1915, in Puerto Rico
Ventura Cofresí, born in 1918 in Puerto Rico
Brigida Cofresí, born in 1920 in Puerto Rico

The direct descendants and family relatives

Roberto Cofresí was the youngest child of Francisco Cofresí (Francesco von Kupferschein) and María Germana Ramírez de Arellano. He had a sister Juana, and two brothers, Juan Francisco and Ignacio. María Germana gave birth to their first daughter, Juana, on the 21st of June of 1785. Two years later, on the 25th of March of 1787 their first son, Juan Francisco, was born, followed by Ignacio, born on the 16th of September of 1789. Juana got married in March

1807 to Germán Colberg, from a rich family in Cabo Rojo. His brother, Juan Francisco, got married in May, 1809 to Juana Balines, also from Cabo Rojo, and Ignacio married María Monserrate del Río in May, 1823.

Juana and Germán had four children. Two of them died very early and the third, a girl, died when she was 21 years old. Only one son, Gabriel Colberg Cofresí, managed to marry and have descendants.

Juan Francisco, Roberto's older brother, had seven children with his wife Juana Balines. Juana María, born in 1810, María de la Cruz, born in 1811, María Magdalena, born in 1813, Nicolas, born in 1817, María Ramona, born in 1819, José Justo, born in 1823, and Juana Josefa, born in 1827. He began his working career as a sailor, as did his brothers Ignacio and Roberto. In 1823, the name of Juan Francisco appears as the captain of a merchant boat owned by Pedro Alacán. After spending some of his early years as a sailor, Juan worked the bulk of his life in the harbor of Cabo Rojo as an employee of José Mendoza, who was godfather to four of his children. The same Mendoza was in charge of the expedition that destroyed the operational base of Roberto Cofresí on Mona Island in 1824. Following this expedition Mendoza became the godfather of the last son of Juan Francisco. The ceremony was held after the execution of Roberto, in 1825.

Ignacio was the captain of the merchant boat Avispa for some time, sailing between Cabo Rojo and San Juan. He had twelve children, and some of them lived during the 20th century. In 1830, Ignacio became one of the largest landowners in the area of Cabo Rojo, where he had many houses and slaves. He died in 1858 and his wife, María Montserrate del Río lived on for 25 more years.

On the 14th of January 1815, Roberto Cofresí married Juana Creitoff, originally from Curacao, when she was only 14 years old. After four years Juana gave birth to their first son. His name was Juan, but he died before he was a year old. One year later Juana gave birth to a daughter, Bernardina. Their third child, a son named Francisco Matías, was born on the 24th of February 1824, but he died from angina pectoris when he was just 4 months old. Juana Creitoff, wife of Roberto Cofresí, lived just one year beyond Roberto's death. She died in May 1826.

The only legitimate child of Roberto Cofresí, Bernardina, married José Estanislao Asencio on the 26th of June 1839 in Cabo Rojo when she was only 18 years old. The couple had eight children, the only grand children of Roberto Cofresí. They were: José Lucas, born on the 18th of September, 1840, María Esterlina, born o the 18th of February, 1842, Antonio Salvador, born on the 13th of June, 1843, Antonio Luciano, born on the 16th of January, 1847, Pablo, born on the 23rd of January, 1849, Isabel Antonia, born on the 1st of November, 1850, María de la Encarnacion, born on the 25th of March, 1853, and finally Juan Bernardo, born on the 27th of May, 1855 (the information comes from the Book of Births (Libro de Matrimonios) Cabo Rojo, no. 5, folio 62).

Roberto Cofresí was known to love his wife and his daughter, but he was also known for romancing other women. It's said that he might have other children outside of his marriage, especially with a beautiful girl named Gisela Amparo who lived in Puerto Juanita, a place Roberto frequently visited. She was the daughter of a local fisherman.

One of the direct descendants was Ana Gonzáles, better known by her married name, Ana Méndez. She was Cofresí's great granddaughter, directly descended from the Cabo Rojo bloodline through her mother, Ana Gonzáles Cofresí. Ana Gonzáles was famous for her interest in education and she was the first member from the Cofresí bloodline to earn high school and university diplomas. She became a teacher and she founded the Puerto Rico High School of Commerce during the 1940's.

Another direct descendant was Severo Colberg Ramírez, a politician who served as a Speaker of the House of Representatives of Puerto Rico during the 1980's. Colberg was also known for his effort to popularize the figure of Cofresí, especially the legends that sprung up after Roberto's death.

While searching for living descendants of Roberto Cofresí, I found several still living in the United States and one in Santo Domingo. His name is Eladio Antonio Cofresí Cabrera; back in 1986, he worked in the city hall of Santo Domingo, the capital of the Dominican Republic.

The myths of Roberto Cofresí

There have been several books written about Roberto Cofresí that are filled with pure fabrication.But it's necessary to dig into all the possible sources, read everything even remotely related with the name of Roberto Cofresí, listen to all the local stories and then try to confirm them, if you want a true picture of the man.

Unfortunately, the same fictional projections occur in a number of books featuring Roberto Cofresí as a principal protagonist, such as the historical novel by Gonzáles Herrera, "La Gloria Llamo Dos Veces" (The Glory Called Twice). He placed our pirate hero, Roberto Cofresí, in a duel with sabers against Juan Pablo Duarte, a national hero of the Dominican Republic, better known as the "Father of the Country". The reason for this imaginary duel centered upon the love of a French woman, Amalia Dupont, who Cofresí supposedly saved from a voodoo ceremony. The author of this novel did not care that Roberto Cofresí was executed by firing squad in Puerto Rico in 1825 and he placed the story to the year of 1842, when Juan Pablo Duarte was preparing for the liberation of the Dominican people from Haitian dominance. Duarte was born in 1813, so he was just twelve years old when Roberto Cofresí was killed.

Apart from these pseudo-historical novels wherein Cofresí was the principal hero, there are a few more books about him, written in a biographical style. Some of the authors of these books did their homework and tried to bring to the public some proven historical information about this famous pirate. A great example would be the book by Enrique Ramírez Brau, "Cofresí, Historia y Genealogia de un Pirata, 1791 – 1825" published in Puerto Rico in 1945. Another is, no doubt, a book published by renowned Puerto Rican historian and author, Walter A. Cardona, "El Marinero, Bandolero, Pirata y Contrabandista Roberto Cofresí (1819-1825)", published in 1991. The author gives us, in 300 pages, the description of Roberto Cofresí as a ruthless killer and smuggler, in dramatic contrast to the Cofresí personae portrayed by most other authors. The latest book written about our pirate comes from Dr. Ursula Schmidt de Acosta, a retired professor from the University of San Juan in Puerto Rico. Dr. Acosta devoted a great deal of time to the research of Cofresí, and in her book, "Cofresí y Ducoudray: Dos Hombres al Margen de la Historia" (Cofresí and Ducoudray: Two Men at the Margin of History), very valuable historical information can be found. Ursula Acosta also wrote another book about this pirate, titled "Quien era Cofresí" (Who was Cofresí).

A great account of the Black Prince of the Caribbean was written by a Puerto Rican author, Roberto Fernandez Valledor. His research was very thorough, including loose ends found in old newspapers and official letters. He published the results of his work in a book titled "El Mito de Cofresí en la Narrativa Antillana", printed in Spanish in 1978. Valledor attempted to distinguish between fact and fiction regarding Cofresí in the folklore of both the Dominican Republic and Puerto Rico.

A classic book about this pirate came from the pen of the famous Puerto Rican historian and author, Alejandro Tapia y Rivera, simply titled "Cofresí".

"El Aguila Negra o Roberto Cofresí – El Terror de los Navegantes" is a story about this pirate with his biographical hints written in 1934 by Bienvenido Camacho, also from Puerto Rico.

The latest book written in Spanish about Roberto Cofresí is also an historical novel, written by Dominican author Ramon Alberto Ferreras, titles "Cofresí el Intrepido", published in Santo Domingo in 1991. Throughout there are many fictional narrations, but part of this book is also dedicated to an historical review of the environment and events in Puerto Rico and the Dominican Republic during Cofresí's era.

There are just two books originating in Puerto Rico or the Dominican Republic dealing with Cofresí that are not written in Spanish. The first, in English, comes from Lee Cooper, and it is titled "Pirate of Puerto Rico". The second, written in German is from German author, Angelika Mectel, and the title is "Das Kurge Heldenhafte Leben Des Don Roberto Cofresí".

Apart from above mentioned books, Roberto Cofresí, and sometimes even his treasure, is mentioned in "Leyendas Puertorriqueñas" of Cayetano Coll and Toste; in different stories published locally, such as "Una Aventura de Cofresí", "El Entierro de Cofresí", or "El Tesoro de la Gruta", published by Nestor Rodríguez Escudero in Puerto Rico in 1971, and in several other books about the history of Puerto Rico, especially in "Historia de Puerto Rico", written by renowned historian Salvador Brau.

The personage of this famous Puerto Rican pirate has also appeared in articles in various newspapers, such as "El Mundo", "El Imparcial", "Puerto Rico Ilustrado", "New York Times" and "US Naval Institute Proceedings".

The figure of Roberto Cofresí Ramírez y Arrellano, the last Caribbean pirate and the "Terror of the Sea" did not escape the attention of moviemakers either. In 1917 and then again in 1919, there were attempts to shoot a movie about this famous pirate. Both attempts started in Puerto Rico and both ended unfinished. The first, directed by Luis Llorens Torres, had the title "El Tesoro de Cofresí" (The Treasure of Cofresí) and it could not be completed because the star of the film, Italian actor Aguiles Zorda, left the island and he never came back. The second attempt, two years later, was the project of Juan Emilio Vigué, with the name of the movie being "La Vida de Cofresí" (The Life of Cofresí). This movie ended unfinished as well, most probably because of financial problems.

Chapter Three

Where to begin the hunt

Some people do not believe that pirates buried their treasure, instead spending their booty on wine and women. While this is certainly the usual case, not all pirates, buccaneers, and corsairs were so short sighted. Some of these characters knew that each passing day might be their last, and as a result, some of them planned ahead with the idea of retiring to a more placid, and legal lifestyle. Subsequently, it only made good sense to hide some of their ill-gotten gains for such eventualities. A prime example would be Henry Morgan who ended up buying a large parcel of land in Jamaica, and becoming governor of that island. He died peacefully in his own bed, surrounded by attending family and servant staff, rather than being hanged or shot to pieces while raising hell on the high seas. Pirates did, in fact, hide their treasure in remote locations where they might retrieve it as needed.

Between 1770 and 1830 there were over 700 foreign merchant ships cruising the Caribbean to and from Europe and America every year. Two of the main Caribbean products were sugar cane and coffee. For example, in 1789, just two years before Roberto Cofresí was born, in Haiti, the half of Hispaniola belonging to the French, there were 451 sugar mills producing 70 million pounds of sugar, and there were 2,810 coffee plantations producing 68 million of pounds of coffee a year. There were also 705 plantations producing wool. Such quantities required many merchant ships for export abroad. All these ships were potential victims of pirates. There were always personal items, jewelry, and ship's money in the captain's cabin to steal aside from the cargo as well.

All the outlaws required a base of operations where they could re-victual their vessels, obtain new crew, tap into local intelligence, and recuperate between their excursions. There were two main pirate bases in the Caribbean; the first was Port Royal in southern Jamaica, and the second was on Tortuga, an island lying along the north side of Haiti. After a short period of domination by the Spanish, the French and the English eventually ruled Tortuga. During the period of French influence, Tortuga became the richest French colony of all because any pirate, corsair, or buccaneer was required to pay a 10% tribute to the governor upon landing at the island. This was a huge tax; therefore, one means of avoiding payment would be to bury their treasure elsewhere before entering the waters of Tortuga. In the case of those corsairs who had letters of marque, their burden was even greater, and they were surcharged for further issues of their patents.

The King of Spain, constantly in a state of war with France, England, or both at one point or another, began issuing his own corso patents. From the mid-1700s these patents were carried by Spanish agents who were primarily interested in French shipping as a prize. These Spanish freebooters operated out of Santo Domingo where they routinely unloaded their booty, and sometimes even the very ships they had attacked were brought into the city for auction. One of the more notable corsairs under Spanish patent at this time was Lorenzo Daniel, aka "Lorencin". Toward the end of the 18th century and into the 19th century, the waters surrounding Hispaniola and Puerto Rico were heavily infested with corsairs of many nations, all with patents of various stripes. To assist Spain in the blockade of the revolting parties of Venezuela, and to quell other contrary subjects in the area, the governor of Puerto Rico, Francisco Gonzales de Linares, issued corso patents in 1822 for the aid and assistance of Spain, along with defense of the local realm. The situation changed drastically a year later when the blockade of Venezuela ended. The corso patents were now obsolete, however, even those that were can-

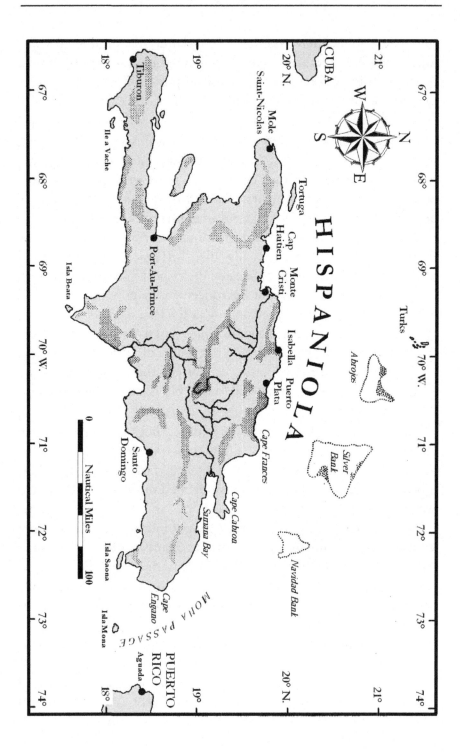

celed meant nothing to the sailors that had taken to the lifestyle of high seas pillaging under their former jurisdiction. This was about the time that Roberto Cofresí began his pirate career. As a youngster, he might have entertained the idea of obtaining his own corso patent, but as that instrument phased out, he was prepared, nonetheless, to take up piracy.

When Roberto Cofresí escaped from the prison of Ozama in Santo Domingo with three confederates in 1824, he unearthed one of his hidden treasures on the beach close to the city of San Pedro de Macoris. All historians agree on this. He definitely did not have any money with him as he escaped prison, so he had to get it somewhere. The only possible explanation is that he just dug up one of his hidden caches. He bought a new boat from local fishermen with this money, and he also bought food and supplies. When he and his fellow escapees arrived in Puerto Rico, he gave each of his companions 10 ounces of gold so that they might have a fresh start in life.

We might also consider that Ignacio Cofresí, Roberto's brother, was a poor man who depended upon Roberto for financial help. Two years after the death of Roberto, Ignacio suddenly became wealthy overnight. Ignacio had served two years in prison as a result of his association with his brother, as Ignacio was the fence Roberto depended upon to convert his stolen booty to cash ashore in Puerto Rico. Ignacio was intelligent: intelligent enough to wait several years after his brother's death before he began spending some of Roberto's hidden loot. When Ignacio Cofresí died in 1858, he was one of the richest men in Puerto Rico, with houses in town, many slaves, and considerable acreage behind his name.

Without a doubt, Roberto Cofresí and his crew had enough treasure to bury. In his short career he successfully looted well over 60 ships. The actual count was probably much higher as not all the ships plundered by Cofresí were recognized as his victims. Here are the names of some which were, without doubt, victims of the Black Prince: merchant ships *El Marayero, Troy, Trush, Bello Narciso, Petronila, Render, La Número 11, Afortunada, Amistad, Superior, La Antenor, Cometa, El Dragon, Hawk, Mercurio, Jones, Eddy, Madre y Familia, Nelsos, Reyner, Altagracia, Rebecca, Ivan, La Fortuna,* brigs *Marte, Catalina, Diego, La Flecha, Aguila,* merchantmen *La Brava*

Criolla, Boniton (English), *Bonne Sophic* (French), *El Cervatillo, D' Hautpoul,* corvette *Flush,* frigates *La Franqueza, Argos, Aurora, Nuestra Señora del Carmen, Palafox, El Aquila, El Pelicano, Polifemo, Saark, Saaveck, San Antonio, Constancia,* and so on.

Walter Cardona, the famous historian and author of Puerto Rico, wrote a book dedicated exclusively to the subject of Roberto Cofresí. Cardona says that after his extensive historical research, he thinks that on many occasions Roberto Cofresí had so much treasure from looted ships that he simply had to leave part of his booty behind with the coastal villagers.

The single surviving member of Roberto Cofresí's crew, his closest friend, Joaquín Hernández, did exactly what his executed captain had planned to do: dig up some buried treasure. Here is an extract from the book "History of Sánchez" (the village of Sánchez, originally known as Las Cañitas, still exists in the bay of Samaná), published around 1982:

"Shortly after 1824 a man by the name of Joaquín Hernández, originally from Spain and residing in Puerto Rico, arrived at Samaná. He was a tall white man with clear eyes who originally worked as a sailor on the boat of the famous pirate from Puerto Rico, Roberto Cofresí y Ramírez de Arellano, who often used numerous hideouts in this bay to confuse his pursuers that were not only American and Spanish ships, but also ships of other nationalities. During of the final pursuit of Cofresí and his crew, Hernández managed to escape without injury and he decided to stay in Samaná and to start living a normal life. Originally a very poor fisherman he shortly became the owner of extensive parcels of land in the area that started at the river Gran Estero and ended approximately in the village of Las Pascualas."

It seems obvious where Joaquín Hernández got his money.

Generally speaking, when trying to associate a place name with a particular person, you examine the identity of villages, towns, geographic names, nick names, government dominions, caves, promontories, and so on. Roberto Cofresí was such a popular namesake in Puerto Rico and the Dominican Republic that you find "Cofresí" associated with many such places today. There is a famous restaurant in Sabana Seca in Puerto Rico called "La Guarida del Pirata Cofresí" and legend claims that one of his treasures is still buried in the caves close to this restaurant.

In the bay of Boqueron, Puerto Rico, where the statue of Roberto Cofresí was erected, there are the remains of a large house that belonged to the rich family of Carbonells back in the 1820s. There are rumors that they were supporters of Roberto Cofresí and he used their property as a hideout. It could be the reason why this place is called "Hacienda Cofresí" yet today. The system of mutually interconnected caves close to this property is widely known as "Cuevas de Cofresí". Other caves bearing the name of the pirate are located around Cabo Rojo, his birthplace. Specifically in the neighborhood of Pedernales, where Roberto Cofresí had his headquarters and where his wife and daughter Bernardina lived. It's said that it was here, where he'd always returned after his successful raids, where he'd hidden some of his treasures. Despite the rumor, no treasure has been found there, at least as far as might be publicly declared, and passage into the cave system is not recommended for a single explorer alone.

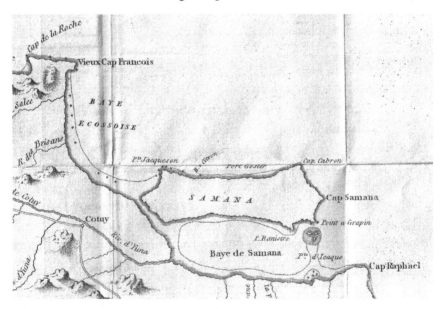

Above: a map of the northeast portion of Hispaniola Island drawn by British cartographer Bryan Edwards, published in 1800. Notice the Samaná peninsula as an island. Courtesy Wiki Commons

One of the most popular and most beautiful beaches on the northern coast of the Dominican Republic, very close to Puerto Plata, is known as "Cofresí beach", where some luxurious hotels were recently erected. There is a cave and a small beach on the south shore, next to the town of San Pedro de Macorís, which is also called the "Beach of Cofresí" and the "Cave of Cofresí". Another cave and some forested areas close to Cabrera on the northern coast also bear the pirate's name; the same as the cave in Sabana del Mar close to Samaná and another one found in the mouth of the Yuma River. Local people quite often named these places after some particular person who visited them regularly. If you see, for example, the name "Cave of Cofresí" there is theoretically a chance that there might be one of his hidden treasures found there.

Other possible places of interest, which could lead to one of the treasures of Roberto Cofresí, are those locales where our pirate spent some time or, even better, where he repeatedly returned from his raids. There are a few in the territory of the Dominican Republic, such as Samaná, Puerto Juanita, a beach called Diamante Beach close to Cabrera or beaches around today's town of San Pedro de Macoris. During the trial of Roberto Cofresí in Santo Domingo on the 3rd of October of 1824 he named some places where he often stopped to share his booty with the local inhabitants.

According to the documents from this trial, he mentioned places such as the village of Mosquito y Sol in the mouth of the river Macoris (it does not exist today), La Romana, locations in the mouth of the river Dulce, of the river Yuma, in Cumayasa, Chavon, the village of Las Cañitas, Sabana del Mar, Matanzas, Nagua, the area of Los Tres Amarras, Sabaneta, Bahía Escocesa, Río San Juan, the beach of Cafemba (today called "Cofresí beach"), Sosua, Maimon, Punta Rusia, Puerto Juanita, Estero Balsa close to Manzanillo, the mouth of the river Nigua, Nizao, Palenque, the beach of Los Almendros, the harbor of Puerto Hermoso, Puerto Viejo and Puerto Tortuguero in the Bay of Ocoa, in Barahona, Gran Estero in Santo Domingo, where he is supposed to have hidden a large amount of loot, and also Petit Trou, Paraiso and Trujin, and other spots along the coast of the Republic of Haiti.

Other folklore sources mention other places, such as Cayos

Levantado in Samaná Bay, consisting of three cays with the most prominent one in the center. In previous years, these cays were known to the locals as "Cayos Rebelde" (Rebel Cays), or Bannister Cays, which denoted an historical event. In 1686, the famous English pirate, Jack Bannister, arrived in Samaná Bay aboard his ship the *Golden Fleece* to careen her. A small French pirate ship, *La Subtille*, under the command of Captain Lagarde joined Bannister there. Bannister sailed there directly from a successful raid along the coast of Venezuela where he'd looted two English merchants. But Bannister's approximate location was known to the Governor of Jamaica, Mollesworth, who immediately sent two war frigates, *HMS Drake* and *HMS Falcon* in pursuit. When Bannister was about to put his ship on the beach, he spotted these two frigates approaching from the entrance to the bay. He immediately placed a battery of his ship's guns on the beach and a famous naval battle ensued. It lasted for almost a day and a night and at the end *Golden Fleece* caught fire and sank, shot up like a piece of Swiss cheese. Some sources state that the English lost 123 men in this battle; meanwhile Bannister only lost about 40 of his men. After *Golden Fleece* went to the bottom the pirates had only one chance to escape by boarding the French pirate ship and sailing to the terminus of the bay where the English frigates could not follow because of their deeper draft. But there was a problem. *La Subtille* could only take on a maximum of 80 persons aboard, so a merciless fight for a spot on the tiny ship began amongst the pirates themselves. The pirates managed to escape, but Jack Bannister's luck did not last long. Just a couple of months later, in January 1687, another English frigate, *HMS Ruby*, finally captured him and returned to the harbor in Jamaica with Bannister hanging on the mast.

Roberto Cofresí most probably was aware of this battle, so it is also highly probable that he would select this uninhabited small island as a place to bury one of his treasures.

Other legends place Cofresí treasures at the Playa Breton, close to the town of Abreu, around Cabo Frances Viejo (Old French Cape), in the vicinity of Samaná peninsula. All these locations of record are potential burial sites of Cofresí's loot.

In Puerto Rico, the undiscovered booty is rumored to be dispersed throughout the beaches on the west coast. The locations are numerous, ranging from Cabo Rojo to Rincón. Specific beaches such as Guajataca, Puerto Herminia, El Ojo del Buey, Pico de Piedra or La Sardinera are mentioned, but specificity generally depends on the place where the stories originate. Cofresí's treasure has been said to be as far north as the Añasco River mouth and as far east as Tamarindo del Sur in Vieques, where fishermen reportedly spotted boxes bound with chains. People have found small quantities of silver and gold coins in Guaniquilla, which is located between Cabo Rojo and Aguada. The discovery of the few coins set off a treasure fever where a larger cache was thought to be hidden nearby.

Mona Island is considered to be a place where several Cofresí treasures can be found. In fact, Mona Island was not only a favorite haunt of Roberto Cofresí: the island attracted such adventurers as Walter Raleigh, Christopher Newport, and Sir Francis Drake. These men explored the island or used it as a base of supply and as place where they waited in ambush for their victims. Even the infamous Captain William Kidd spent ten days here in 1699 before his final journey to Boston. As yet no one has determined what William Kidd was doing on Mona Island for those ten days. Of course, there are rumors that he hid part of his huge treasure in one of the numerous caves on Mona Island, because when he finally arrived in Boston, only a small portion of this treasure, looted from Muslim ships in the Indian Ocean was to be found aboard his ship. He had to hide this treasure somewhere in the Caribbean, because he sailed from Mona Island to the south of Hispaniola Island, where he burnt his ship *Queddah Merchant,* supposedly near the shore of Catalina Island, and purchased a much smaller schooner, the *Antonio* from fishermen in the town of La Romana. He then sailed to Boston with this schooner.

One of the treasures supposedly hidden by Cofresí on Mona Island, mentioned several times in different historical documents, should be buried on the beach of Uvero. A detailed description of this treasure can be found in the book of Arsenio S. Martin titled "Isla de Mona es Isla de Tesoros" (Mona Island is Treasure Island), published in 1937. According to Martin, Cofresí boarded an English merchant ship sailing between Santo Domingo and Puerto Rico and he looted her cargo, which consisted of several iron chests full of golden coins. Roberto then sailed to Mona Island and went to Uvero beach and buried his treasure close by. He marked the spot with some logs of an old leafy tree, close to the well known as "Ojo de Agua" and added some other signs as references. Unfortunately, over time these indicators have been erased and the treasure remains hidden. Nevertheless several expeditions went to Mona Island between 1930 and 1940, in search of Cofresí treasure and they actually found some buried coins in a jar with a skull nearby, and some other skeletons in another location, along with some jewelry. But they could not prove that these treasures were part of the booty that Roberto Cofresí had hidden on the island.

Walter Cardona, renowned Puerto Rican author and historian, wrote a report wherein he described the expedition to Mona Island of 1957. The purpose of this expedition, lead by Richard Winner, was to search for buried treasures on the island. Mr. Winner, author of "Triangulo del Demonio II", indeed found a small treasure on the beach. The treasure consisted of gold and silver coins and it was buried in ceramic jars. Interestingly enough, the treasure was discovered together with a human skull. Taking into account the stories about the habit of Cofresí to kill some of his companions in order to throw their bodies over the treasure to guard it, this discovery was immediately considered as one of the possible treasures of Roberto Cofresí. It's also possible that the skull belonged to Roberto's friend and crew member, Pepe Cartagena, who was killed during an incident on Mona Island.

There are a number of stories regarding the Cofresí treasures where one of his confederates was killed and buried with the treasure, purportedly to raise a spirit that would guard the loot. Sometimes just the head of the unfortunate was placed with the treasure, other times, the entire corpse. Allegedly, Cofresí buried one of his fallen comrades with some treasure after boarding a ship in Aguada. The spot was beneath a palm tree, which has yet to be found.

Legends also claim Cofresí always buried his cache in a large chest bound with chains, which he would throw into the sea. The chains were made of gold, and when anyone approached the chest, the sea would become rough.

Some of the folk legends orbiting the ghost of Roberto Cofresí are absurd to say the least... among these, a claim that a chest containing the loot was hidden in the water under a tree and that it was only visible with the direct light of a full moon. According to this legend, the treasure was guarded by a school of fish constantly swimming around it to keep it disguised under the murky water. These fish were also capable of transforming into sharks, devouring any one that approached the treasure when there was no moonlight.

In Cabo Rojo, folklore claims that Cofresí treasure might be buried at the end of an anchor chain, but that when trying to pull it out with bulls, the animals wouldn't budge as they sensed the presence of death nearby. Another folklore story claims that at Poza Clara in Isabela there was a large cache, however the only way to reach it was to sacrifice a newborn at the site, an action that would cause the water to part and allow access to the area. Some legends suggest that Cofresí was reincarnated in another body after dying in order to guard his treasures.

Another suspect locality where one might expect to find Cofresí treasure could be those places where Cofresí waited to ambush his victims. This might have been, for example, Beata Island, or the island of Alto Velo on the southern coast of the Dominican Republic, or Maimon, Puerto Plata, Montecristi, or Cabo Francés on the northern coast.

To make the best of time and resources, it's necessary to winnow out the ridiculous rumors and concentrate on the more probable stories when a hunt for treasure begins. One of the most fabled and repeated stories centers upon the anchor chain leading from shore, seaward. People call it the "Cofresí Chain", claiming that where it appears, it will lead to a Cofresí treasure. Unfortunately the chain always starts buried on the beach and goes to the sea. Sometimes it appears and then disappears again. When you want to touch it, you cannot. One could say — local myth, nothing more, but the same myth is told in about twelve different coastal towns of the Dominican Republic, all of them on the northern coast of the island. I visited almost all of them trying to get some more information about this mysterious chain. I could not find anybody who had seen "the chain" until I arrived at Punta Rusia, a small, remote fishing village between Luperon and Montecristi on the northern coast of the island. I spoke to several fishermen and they told me the same story with the exception that there are two persons that have seen this chain during the last few years. I located one of them, an empathetic Italian fellow named Tony, who has lived there with his Dominican family for more than 12 years. He was a diver and he repeated the story and described the place when he saw it. But he only saw it twice. He has not been able to find it since. Tony is not a person who would impress a person with cheap stories; he does not need to. The chain was buried on the beach in the surf and when he followed it, it disappeared after almost 100 meters in the depths. He never discovered the end of the chain, nor what might have been attached to it. Tony had never heard about Cofresí and the chain legend. He was simply looking for shipwrecks there to serve as a place of interest for his diving clients and he was sure that this anchor chain would lead him to one.

Of course, the most important piece of information was the location where the chain had been seen. It was very close to the former village known as Puerto Juanita, a place that Roberto Cofresí often visited. He had a girl friend there and most probably some descendents too. One legend says that he buried at least two treasures on the beach there. It is historically proven that he frequently shared his

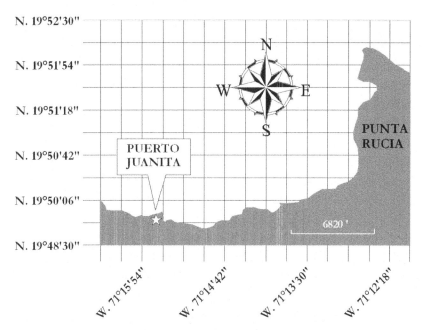

booty with villagers. In exchange they repaired his pirate ship that finally wrecked and burned in the bay in front of Puerto Juanita. The legends about the buried treasures of Roberto Cofresí occasionally claim that he always left hints so that he could retrieve these treasures when needed, which included, for example, planting recognizable trees nearby. Other accounts list other distinctions, including a series of silver medallions engraved with the initials "R.C." or a chain that emerged from the sea and went into the jungle.

Regarding the above-mentioned medallion, there is a story that seems to be true, because it gives us dates and real names. A Dominican author of history books, Ramon Alberto Ferreras, writes in his historical novel about Roberto Cofresí, that a musician named Juan Mendoza Mieses lived in the coastal town of San Pedro de Macoris, close to Santo Domingo, back in 1919. It's said that Mieses owned a strange coin, or medallion, engraved on one side. It bore the image of a barrel with a rising sun with entrance to a cave and a chain close to the barrel. There were also the initials R.C. on the lower part of this design. He mentioned this coin to a friend, Jose Olmos, a watchmaker from the same town. Mieses came to his house one night with another man by the name of Zachary Phill, a chemist working in a sugar mill known as "Cristobal Colon" in the same city, who owned a similar coin, featuring some strange codes and the same initials. The three men were sure that these two coins are the key to the location of a treasure buried by Cofresí. They all knew the legend about the supposed treasure of this pirate, buried on Playa Marota, close to the city of San Pedro de Macoris. They agreed to go there at night to dig it up. While Mendoza was approaching to the planned rendezvous point, he overheard the conversation of his two companions, devising a plan to kill him after they dug up the treasure. Mendoza panicked, ran home fearing for his life and that of his whole family, and flushed the coin down the toilet. Much later, his daughters, Consuelo, Caridad and Carmelita, verified that their father once owned a coin of Roberto Cofresí. We find some slight credibility for this story as city archives and church registry records, document Juan Mendoza Mieses, a musician, as actually living in the city of San Pedro de Macoris in 1919.

Next, I made a list of all the possible places where Roberto Cofresí could hide his treasures and eliminate those where such treasure was later actually found. The prime example could be the area of small cays in Samaná Bay because the only survivor of Cofresí's crew, Joaquín Hernández, lived there and "suddenly became rich". It was the common opinion that he got his vast fortune from digging up some of the treasure of his former pirate captain. The chest with gold coins and jewelry found on the bottom of the Yuma River is another example that should be cast out. Sometime in the after a prolonged rainy period, the wild waters of Yuma River expelled most of the delta at its mouth, exposing the lid of a chest hidden until then. It so happened that a local fisherman saw it, opened the chest and he found gold. He was so happy that he got drunk the same evening in the local pub and there he told the whole story to his friends. This was during the severe regime of dictator Leonidas Trujillo Molina in the Dominican Republic and, as a result the next day the fisherman was arrested and he had to reveal the location of the chest to the local police commander, who went immediately to check the story himself. According to the detailed description of the fisherman, he found the chest with the treasure and recovered it. The next morning both treasure and police commander disappeared.

In the southern region of La Romana close to the Dulce River, a family was having a house built and as the cellar was being excavated, workers found a small coffer filled with silver and gold coins, dated between 1819 and 1823. Considering that Cofresí appeared in the area frequently, coupled with the coin dates, this may very well prove to be a Cofresí treasure cache, albeit unproven.

Following his dramatic capture, Cofresí was jailed with some of his crew in the town of Guayama. Roberto was held there for three days prior to being sent to a more substantial prison in San Juan. While being treated for his wounds under the supervision of the mayor of Guayama, Cofresí begged for a private conversation with the mayor. Records indicate that Cofresí offered the mayor a bribe of 4000 pesos for his release. This was a very large offer as it corresponds to an equivalent of 31.25 pounds of silver. However, the mayor, a man by the name of Brenes, feared the wrath of the governor, and turned down the bribe, especially since Cofresí had escaped previously. Obviously, Cofresí had the money somewhere.

In 1889, the Puerto Rican, Francisco Carlos Ortea published a book titled "El tesoro de Cofresí" (Treasure of Cofresí), wherein he states that a small group of adventures pursued the legend of the treasures buried by Roberto Cofresí and actually found one. The source of the author's information has never been confirmed, but we might give it some attention, particularly pages 179 -181, where he describes in detail what this group of young treasure hunters supposedly found, to wit:

"The treasure consisted of thirty-two ceramic jars. Twenty-eight were full of gold and silver coins and in the remaining four jars there were pieces of antique jewelry. Here is the complete list of what was found:

ITEMS	*VALUE*
• - *Spanish gold coins 8 escudos* .... *3,676 pesos*	
• - *American gold coins of 8 escudos*....................... *8,512 pesos*	
• - *Spanish gold coins of 4 escudos* .... *1,085 pesos*	
• - *Doubloons of 4* .... *1,164 pesos*	
• - *American coins of 10 Dollars* .... *3,650 pesos*	
• - *American coins of 5 Dollars* .... *8,215 pesos*	
• - *Various large foreign gold coins* .... *3,656 pesos*	
• - *Various small foreign gold coins* .... *4,505 pesos*	
• - *Different stamped pieces*...................................... *4,672 pesos*	
• - *Doubloons* .... *18,306 pesos*	
• - *Total value of coins* .... *452,974 pesos*	
• - *Total value of jewelry* .... *26,345 pesos*	
• - *Total value of the treasure* .... *479,319 pesos"*	

The problems with finding the 'right' place to begin searching for Cofresí treasure is hinged upon history itself — many things have happened during the 190 years since Cofresí 's death. Some deserted

Above: the author is seen here with an ancient anchor at a small fishing village along the northern coast of the Dominican Republic.

areas are now streets, villages, and towns where it is impossible to dig and search. Quiet beaches are now full of tourists and hotels, and the physical coastline in areas of interest has also drastically changed on several occasions. A prime example is the area around Playa Diamante (Diamond Beach), where we know that Cofresí was a frequent visitor. There was a small mangrove island in the bay near this beach where Roberto used to anchor his ship before going to shore. The legend says that he buried at least one huge treasure in the vicinity of this beautiful, deserted beach. The problem is that this beach and its surroundings were completely destroyed and its topography has been changed forever after a huge earthquake and tsunami that killed over 2,000 inhabitants and erased three coastal villages from the map. This happened in the 1940s. Playa Diamante exists today, but the beach has a completely different shape and the small mangrove island inside the bay no longer exists.

Physical landmarks play a large part in the treasure discovery process. Cofresí always buried his treasure somewhere that had particular features he could remember, such as oddly shaped trees, clusters of palms, near an outcrop or notable rock, or within caves. Obviously he had no desire to spend a great deal of time trying to find his own loot; when he needed money, it was usually an immediate need. But the profile of the coast has changed over the last nineteen decades and these features might be lost forever. Therefore, an approximate locale is not sufficient. You might spend a lifetime searching every square meter of a suspect beach. A cave offers similar problems... is the treasure in the cave, or outside of it? One must be able to imagine what a location might have looked like 200 years ago. There are many questions, many potential hiding places, and few supporting facts. But if you do not look, you will not find any treasure!

Montecristi

The area of Montecristi is famous for pirates and sunken ships. One of the principal reasons was the fact that the most famous pirate hangout of all time, Tortuga Island, is just 55 miles west of Montecristi. Many well-known corsairs, buccaneers, and pirates cruised these waters looking for their victims over the past centuries, and Roberto Cofresí y Ramírez de Arellano was among them.

Spanish conquistadors converted the little village of Montecristi into a larger Spanish settlement by 1506 and in 1533 Montecristi was declared a province by Sir Juan de Bolaños who migrated there with sixty other families from the Canary Islands. Twelve years later the

Above: the famous "El Morro" mountain as seen on the horizon, an unmistakeable mark on the shore in front of Montecristi.

Spanish crown recognized Montecristi as a city but prosperity did not last: most of the inhabitants moved to nearby Bayaya (today a territory of Haiti) and gradually mixed themselves with the inhabitants of Puerto Real. By the end of the 16th century destiny smiled on this city again when Montecristi was separated from Puerto Real and came to be one of the most important harbors for the Spaniards on the whole island of Hispaniola. It had gradually become an important trading port by the 19th century, mainly exporting sugar, mahogany and other crops for European trade. But the riches flowing constantly through this port were not always the result of legitimate business. On the contrary – the biggest business in Montecristi at that time came from smuggling.

During its heyday Montecristi was known as a center for contraband commerce and several hundred ships called on its harbor annually. Many of these vessels came from British North America, where European-imposed laws forbade trade with either the French or the Spanish. Still others came from islands elsewhere in the Caribbean. Spanish law denied any, but Spanish vessels, from trading in its colonies, and this has resulted in little documentation regarding vessels loading or unloading in Monticristi. Residents of Hispaniola and

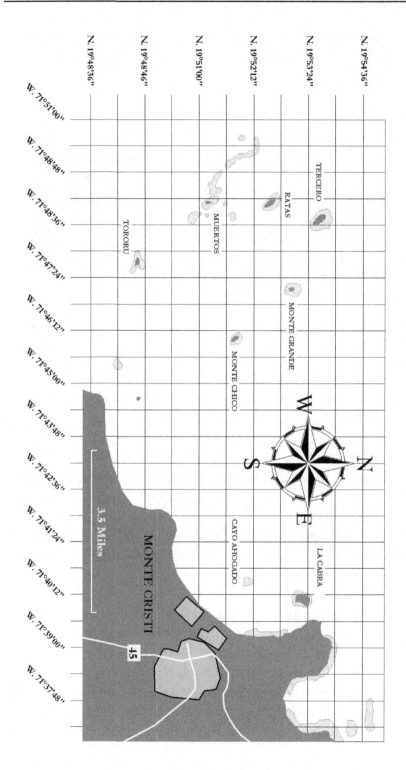

other places on the Spanish Main used Montecristi to satisfy their needs as consumers, despite the imperial restrictions placed upon them by those in the metropolitan areas.

The Bay of Montecristi is an extremely dangerous place for maritime shipping even today. Especially the area of the 'Seven Brothers' a group of islands, which is literally festooned with shipwrecks of all imaginable types and vintages. The sea bottom suddenly rises from 90 feet to the surface and the coral plateau around these seven small sandy cays has an average depth of only 10-15 feet. There are many unmarked and dangerous coral heads in the area that rest just below the surface at low tide, forming deadly traps for even the smallest boats. Some of the wrecks have already been located and positively identified, while others, known to be wrecked here, are yet to be found. And, of course there are many others, which are unknown, wrecks waiting to be discovered. This has been the case for centuries.

These cays were there when Christopher Columbus first arrived in the Montecristi area. He was the first person who made a chart of this bay depicting the 'Seven Brothers' within the bay.

There are some pirate shipwrecks in the bay. One of them lies in shallow waters in front of Cayo Tercero, one of the famous Seven Brothers. There is a huge coral plateau with a depth of between three and five meters (approximately twelve to twenty feet) in front of Cayo Tercero. If the water is dirty in the bay, which is always the case after a heavy rain, crystal clear water can always be found around this small cay. The sea bottom here is primarily rocky with massive coral formations sometimes reaching almost to the sea's surface. These features are intermingled with sandy pockets and patches of sea grass. Dangerous, razor sharp coral heads stand an eternal watch just below the water on the west side of the key. These reefs sounded a death knell for at least two ships, which were impaled upon them.

About eighty meters (260 feet) from the sandy beach on the south side of Cayo Tercero there are six huge iron cannon and two anchors. The first lot consists of four cannon, which are quietly resting on the sea bottom, two of them almost touching one another. A huge anchor ring protrudes from the coral formation about forty feet from them. There was another cannon in shallow water at a depth of about three feet a couple of years ago but, that cannon was removed by local fishermen.

The main reason why the remains of this specific wreck are thought to be that of a pirate ship is the fact that each cannon is different. A

Above: another view of "El Morro".

mix of guns was common on pirate ships, unlike commercial vessels which were normally fitted with complimentary guns and cannon shot that could be used at any station on the deck. Pirates, corsairs, and buccaneers frequently commandeered the guns of their victims. As a result, an assortment of cannon were found on pirate vessels of different calibers and makes. The remains are spread, heavily in-crusted with coral, throughout a range of almost one hundred and fifty meters, indicating a violent end.

My first conjecture was that Cofresí had buried one of his caches on one or more of these sandy cays. However, upon paying them a visit, I discovered this would hardly be the case since none of them had any attributes that could be a key to relocation of any such buri-al. There are no big rocks, trees or odd stones. In fact there is very little vegetation... only sand. How would Cofresí know where he interred his treasure? Furthermore, there is no cover, and anybody might see him digging during daylight, and approach to any of these little islands would be suicidal during the hours of darkness.

The only exception was the key known as Isla Cabra. It is only several hundred meters from the mainland shore. It was used as an anchorage for Christopher Columbus' ships, which anchored there for four days in January of 1493. It is the largest of the Seven Brothers and unlike the others, there are trees and vegetation growing on it. Nowadays there are salt ponds in the center of this small island.

I spent almost an entire day searching for some clue on this island. The only visible sign is a ruin of an old lighthouse, but it was built there long after Roberto Cofresí died. There are sharp rocks on the side of the island facing the open sea and a sandy beach on the side facing the mainland. My metal detector was useless there because of tons of metal scraps, bottle caps, old cans and nails. The small beach on Isla Cabra has been a favorite weekend spot for decades.

I did not want to give up so easily. All the documents that I studied regarding the Cofresí treasures mentioned the area of Montecristi as one of the spots where he hid some of his treasure. But where?

Taking into account that westward of Montecristi, in the direction of Manzanillo, are sandy beaches while on the opposite side of El Morro only inaccessible mangroves are found, the treasure should

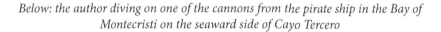

Below: the author diving on one of the cannons from the pirate ship in the Bay of Montecristi on the seaward side of Cayo Tercero

Above: Isla Cabra as seen from the mainland.

be somewhere toward the east, on the way to Punta Rusia and Puerto Plata. There is a road from Montecristi that goes alongside the shore in this direction. This dusty road does not exactly follow the shore, but the road goes close enough to make inspection of the shore convenient. There are numerous footpaths the locals use to get from the road to the beach.

The coastline is mainly rocky, punctuated occasionally with patches of mangroves. Then a long sandy beach came into view. The map displayed the name "Punta Mangle". There was a path to the beach from the main road (if we can call it a main road) so turned and went there. The beach was full of empty pink conch shells, evidently brought there by local fishermen. An old boat, punctured with many holes lay on the beach, but there was nobody around. The beach was partly covered with sea grass, but no significant rock or lone tree was in sight. After some time wandering about I decided to follow the road.

More small beaches followed, but with the same result — no signs showing the way to some buried treasure. If there had been some, over time, storms, winds and waves had already erased them. Next stop was a small fishing village, Buen Hombre. It clearly resembled Punta Rusia, sans tourist. On both sides of the village, whose bay was

full of small fishing boats, knonwn locally as 'yolas', there were mangroves with their innumerable channels, passages and inner lakes.
I knew that the same scenery would continue to Punta Rusia, and
then further, to La Isabela, Maimon and Puerto Plata.

Above: Punta Mangle beach.

Though dissatisfied, I put another black X on my "Cofresí Treasure
Map", packed my stuff, and as the last rays of the sun fell on the horizon, I slowly started my way back home.

Puerto Juanita

The north shore of the Dominican Republic west of Puerto Plata
remains unspoiled and beautiful; particularly the vast area between
Monticristi and La Isabela Bay. This stretch of coast is about 90%
mangroves, much of which reaches inland for 60 kilometers. This
impenetrable mass of vegetation is infrequently dotted with small
beaches and rocky outcrops. The mangroves, mainly the Red variety,

hide waterways that meet in hidden lakes, which are fascinating.

Mangroves grow very quickly and they can completely obscure beaches in a few years. They've slowly swallowed small islands in the past and forced numerous fishing villages to move inland over time. This was the case with Puerto Juanita about 150 years ago. The small beach in front of a few simple cottages made from palm trees had been slowly but constantly overtaken by mangroves and one day the elders decided to move their living quarters about one kilometer inland. The village, now called Estero Balsa, lives its quiet life just as it did 150 years ago. Men go early in the morning about 6 kilometers to the closest coastal village of Punta Rusia to fetch their fishing boats and sail away. Every day there are fewer fish to bring back home, so most of young people have been looking for other jobs to make a decent living. On the weekends they sit together playing dominos and talking about the past, present and future, about the hopes and despairs of their daily life. Sometimes they recall stories of their grandfathers regarding pirates and buried treasure. The principal hero of these stories and legends has almost always been Roberto Cofresí.

Above: mangroves in front of the former Puerto Juanita.

As I sat with them sharing a bottle of "Presidente", a famous local beer, they also remembered a big rock in the small bay - or better said what remains of this bay after mangrove expansion - that could still be seen in 1986. This rock had always been known as "La Piedra de Cofresí" (Cofresí Rock) because he supposedly tied his ship there during his frequent visits to this community. The rock finally disintegrated and its smaller parts were washed away by waves during last twenty years. The remnants of a small pier were still visible underwater in the late 80´s. Today there's just a narrow channel that leads between two massive mangrove hammocks to the former beach.

Above: Entrance to some of the numerous mangrove channels in the area of the former Puerto Juanita.

This channel is so narrow and shallow that it can only be navigated with a kayak. The only visitors are sea birds and small fish. The time when manatees and sea turtles could be seen here are long gone. At the entrance into the mangroves the water is so shallow at low tide that even a kayak must be emptied and pushed forward by hand.

The ideal base for research of Puerto Juanita is, no doubt, Punta Rusia, laying just a couple of miles to east. Not so long ago, Punta

Rusia was a quiet, lazy, small fishing village. But this is not the case now. About ten years ago an older German entrepreneur from Puerto Plata decided to use a small sandy island that lies about two miles from shore and five miles from the village as a daily destination for the generally bored tourists from the Puerto Plata resort complex of Playa Dorada. He started with two small boats and one bus; today there are over 20 tourist boats and sometimes his company handles over 300 tourists per day. "Cayo Paraiso", or "Paradise Island" became the number one tourist excursion of the entire northern coast.

Fortunately, nobody has any interest at all in the coast full of mangroves, so my investigation was completely undisturbed from the beginning to the end. I decided to spend several days there, trying to find out where the original beach of Puerto Juanita was located 190 years ago. It was on that beach where Roberto Cofresí was supposed to have buried at least one of his famous treasures. He visited this small fishing community quite often. It's said that his descendents are still walking there among the inhabitants of the village of Estero Balsa.

Above: Paradise Island (Cayo Paraiso)

I found the remains of the original pier of Puerto Juanita at the bottom of the entrance to the channel, but that was all I found. After a whole day searching by kayak in narrow channels around that spot, and sometimes climbing among the thick mangroves branches, I had to admit that there is no way to find it. The sea and the mangroves covered everything over many years ago.

But there was something else of interest to find there. According to the Dominican researcher Ramon Alberto Ferreras, the author of the only book about Cofresí published in the Dominican Republic, titled "Cofresí, El Intrepido" (Cofresí the Intrepid), published in Santo Domingo in 1992, Roberto Cofresí lost his ship *El Aguila Negro* precisely in front of Puerto Juanita. He was supposed to have burned her in the bay because he did not need her any more. He captured a larger and more suitable ship in the south of the island and he towed his lovely *El Aguila Negro* to Puerto Juanita where he put her to final rest on the sea bottom. How Roberto Cofresí took possession of this ship remains a mystery today. According to some rumors he took this ship as prey; according to the others he supposedly bought *El Aguila Negro* in Cuba. Whatever the case, it was worthy of investigation.

The best way to get information in this case was to sit down with the old local fishermen, drink some beer together and start asking questions. The necessary result came to me on the first evening of drinking with them. There was supposed to be a fisherman who found an old anchor precisely in front of the former Puerto Juanita harbor a couple of years ago. The best part was that I was told that this anchor is still there, standing as a decoration in a small family hotel called "La Tortuga" at the entrance of Punta Rusia.

I went there the next morning and the anchor was indeed there. The strange thing was that both the local fishermen and the owner of the hotel were absolutely sure that this specific anchor belonged to the lost ship of pirate Roberto Cofresí. When I asked them why they think so, they answered they simply know it is true.

So, I took my diving gear, hired a local fisherman with his boat and went to search the sea bottom in front of the pier. It was very shallow, full of sand and sea grass and occasional coral heads. After several dives and three days spent swimming in lines I was sure that if there is a shipwreck, it must be buried deep under the sand or lost far away among the channels. There was absolutely no hint there. My underwater metal detector went silent for all three days apart from two beer bottle caps. The old fisherman who found the anchor unfortunately died a short time ago so he could not show me the exact place where he found the anchor. But I am still convinced that the rest of *El Aguila Negro* lies under the sand in the bay, and the buried chests full of gold and jewelry Roberto Cofresí buried on the beach of the original Puerto Juanita site, might be somewhere under the mangroves as well.

Above: Punta Rusia sunset.

Before I left Punta Rusia, I decided to speak with Tony, an Italian diver, who was alleged to have seen the famous "Cofresí chain" with his own eyes. I found Tony working in his house, which sat a dozen meters from the beach. He is a nice guy, always smiling, pleasant and willing to share his experience. He has been living in Punta Rusia for more than ten years. When I asked him, he told me everything that he knew about the chain.

A few years ago Tony was hunting for some coral formations where he might bring some of his SCUBA clients the following day. At the time he was about 200 meters from shore when he spotted a chain leading seaward in about 12 meters of crystal clear water. He began following it out to sea, thinking, at first, that it was simply an old boat chain. As the depth increased he lost sight of the chain in the depths. Being a man of action, Tony donned his dive gear and dove to the bottom in 28 meters of water where he found the chain once more and continued to follow it. The chain was so long that he could not see the end of it, and he followed it to a depth of 37 meters before he returned to his boat. The chain followed the seafloor ever further out. Very strange. Tony had no GPS, something he would later regret.

The following day, Tony returned to find the chain, which he did, and continued his exploration further to a depth of 42 meters. Still there was no end to the chain and it became buried in the seafloor. Where did the chain come from? Where did it end? It was a mystery.

There was no anchor to be found... another mystery! Just this rusty, old heavy ship's chain lost in the deep. Why?

Returning to the village, Tony began making inquiries of the local fishermen as to the chain, and what it had been attached to. Nobody had any answers save one old fisherman who told Tony the chain was cursed and that he should leave it alone, otherwise he would go insane for the remainder of his life. The fisherman was serious. Tony paid him no heed and returned to the chain's location the following day. There was a problem: he could not find the chain. He searched for several days thereafter but could not find it, knowing all the while that the chain was too large to have been removed from its resting place. He never saw it again. As he stared seriously at my face, he admitted that the chain might, in fact, be cursed. He did not understand the situation. He was not smiling.

Punta Inglesa Beach

The southern region of the Dominican Republic, around Barahona city is famous for its numerous historic shipwrecks. During the first decades of the Conquest of the New World, the southern side of Hispaniola was the obligatory route for the treasure laden Spanish galleons. They had to lay over in Santo Domingo, the first metropolis of the Spanish overseas empire. The royal clerks were there waiting for the cargo manifests of these ships, to check the cargo, store some treasure or offload the cargo to others ships before vessels departed for Cadiz. Santo Domingo gradually lost its unique administrative position to Havana, where the fleets were gathered twice a year prior to departure for Spain. The fleets traveled from Havana to Spain in groups protected by warships to repel pirates. Galleons attacked by the pirates were looted and then sent to the bottom. Spanish monarchs, having lost a great deal of treasure to the pirates, formed convoys, known as "flotas", with supporting vessels that were heavily armed to protect the merchantmen in route to Spain. This tactic greatly reduced the loss of treasure to pirates.

Even so, many single merchant ships, especially from other countries, sailed the waters all around the Hispaniola Island every year and Santo Domingo, though no longer the head quarters of Spain in the New World, still played a very important role as a huge international merchant harbor. According to statistics, literally several hundred ships sank in and around the Santo Domingo harbor since the beginning of the Spanish Conquest. Most of these losses were due to hurricanes. Also, Ocoa Bay, less than one hundred kilometers west of Santo Domingo, was used as an alternative harbor for both Spanish galleons and smaller merchant ships alike. The deep sheltered bay with a fine wharf occasionally offered more facilities than were to be found at the overcrowded Santo Domingo harbor. There was another reason to put in at Ocoa Bay: there were no strict Spanish crown rules nor officious clerks to be found there, therefore illicit business was much easier to conduct at Ocoa than was the case in Santo Domingo.

Marine traffic on the southern coast of Hispaniola passed by Cape Tiburon, Beata Island, and the island of Alto Velo while heading toward the Mona Passage, where ships bound for Europe would turn north and strike out for the open Atlantic. From the time of Henry Morgan and Francis Drake, these waters were a favorite place to wait in ambush for passing merchant ships. Henry Morgan had a base in Ille a Vache in Haitian territory, not too far from Beata Island. And Roberto Cofresí continued to hold with this strategy as he waited for his victims in these waters as well. It's been confirmed that he spent some time waiting for passing ships in Beata Island and Alto Velo

Island coming ashore in that region many times.

There is a beautiful, small, deserted beach, in front of Beata Island, which is just about five miles from the mainland. This beach is called Punta Inglesa, and it lies between Barahona and Pedernales. Legend says that Roberto Cofresí buried one of his treasures at the extreme end of this beach. He was very popular in this area and many stories can be heard about him yet today in Barahona and the surrounding countryside. Several local historians regale his exploits and his generosity toward the poor local inhabitants who loved him. The reason many people in this region believe that Cofresí buried some of his treasure on that beach is the fact that in the past there were some conins found on Punta Inglesa beach, as well as another beach close by known as Cienaga Beach.

An historian from Barahona, Matías Ramírez, claims that Roberto Cofresí abandoned an old cannon that he no longer needed, on Punta Inglesa Beach. The cannon was found by local fishermen and supposedly it is the same iron cannon that is on display at the malecon (ocean avenue) in Barahona today. For many Cofresí devotees, this is reason enough to believe that he also buried some treasure on this beach. Several years ago fishermen found some old French coins and gold jewelry in the sand of this same beach after a strong storm.

Today the city of Barahona, officially known as Santa Cruz de Barahona, is a sleepy town. It is located about 200 kilometers west of the capital of Santo Domingo and it has around 90,000 of inhabitants. There is a small harbor where medium size cargo ships arrive from time to time, principally to load the cement from the local mines. The international company, CEMEX, is the largest industry in the region. Apart from that, Barahona residents and those folks in the surrounding area make their living from agriculture, livestock, precious larimar stone mines, and a slowly increasing tourism industry. Barahona also has a nice airport, but almost no aircraft use it. The region, in spite of all the promises of the government, especially concerning tourism, seems to live in oblivion.

Riding west towards the much smaller town of Pedernales, very close to the Haitian border, you will pass many really beautiful beaches. After Barahona the beaches are sandy, but further west as you approach the Haitian border, they are more frequently covered with stones, instead of sand. The most famous beach in the area, Bahia de las Aguilas (Bay of the Eagles), considered one of the most beautiful beaches on the whole island, lies close to Cabo Rojo. Our Punta Inglesa beach is close to the beach known as Cienaga, closer to Barahona. Generally it does not appear on the map, being too small and infrequently visited, and then only by the occasional fisherman.

Above: the beautiful beach of San Rafael close to Barahona.

Arriving at Punta Inglesa beach, I was quite disappointed. Steep stonewalls surrounded the beach, there was no white sand, and I could not see any vegetation at all. No old tree to use as a marker, no prominent rocks, nothing like that. I followed a tiny dusty path that curved among the rocks, leading down to the beach. The sound of breaking waves was tremendous and I could not imagine a small boat trying to pass through the surf and land on the beach. Wherever I looked, I could not find any location where Cofresí would bury his treasure. But in spite of that, old Spanish and French coins have been found among the stones on this beach along with some gold jew-

Above: Approach to Punta Inglesa beach.

elry. There was only one explanation that crossed my mind. All these finds came from some shipwreck lying close by. The waves, storms and constant currents could transport some of the coins from the sea bottom and throw them onto the beach.

Regardless, I walked the beach up and down. It did not take long... the Punta Inglesa beach is not very big. The beach is closed at both ends by high white rocks.

The configuration of the coast could have changed during the past two hundred years. However these rocks were definitely here at the time Roberto Cofresí was sailing these waters lurking behind them waiting for his victims.

After some time I decided that there was no location here that could be remotely considered as a possible hiding place for some treasure, unlike other places I had already visited. So I started to climb back to the dusty road where I left my car. When I reached the top, I put another black X on my map. "Keep looking", I thought to myself.

Samaná Bay

Samaná Bay and its surroundings was a favorite hangout for Roberto Cofresí. He spent many summer holidays there during his childhood, part of his family lived there, his best friend Joaquín Hernández was from there, and Roberto knew the mangrove channels, lakes, and rivers like the palm of his hand. His pirate career started there and he came back to Samaná regularly throughout his life. Also, on more than one occasion his knowledge of the hidden water passages, channels and mangrove traps in the area saved him prom capture by Spanish war ships. There are several legends claiming that in this specific area Cofresí buried not one, but several of treasures. No doubt, after my bad luck in Puerto Juanita and the Montecristi area on the north and the Playa Inglesa area in the south of the island, my hopes were focused on this promising search area.

Samaná or Xamaná is a word coming from the language of the original Indian inhabitants of the island and arguments among academicians about the meaning of this word continue to this day. Authors Don Narciso and Alberti Bosch, in their history book titled "Apuntos para la pre-historia de Quisqueya" (Remarks for the pre-history of Quisqueya) assure us that the name "Samaná" is of Phoenician origin and means "…. the place where the Chief from Carthage known as Zamora once arrived…" The original inhabitants called their island "Quisqueya". Bosh also found a sculptured head with a beard on a rock at the entrance to the cave known as "Caño Hondo". He interpreted this image as a Phoenician semblance of the

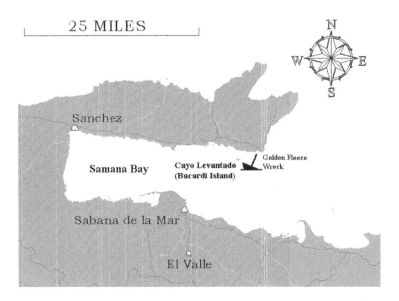

god Hercules and determined it as the proof that Phoenician sailors visited this place almost 3,000 years ago.

The Samaná Peninsula, situated in the northeast of the Dominican Republic has a very rich history. Across from Samaná Bay there are ancient subterranean caves, many of which still preserve anthropomorphic representations. Indigenous people lived in this area before Christopher Columbus arrived in 1492. Unlike peaceful Taino Indians that inhabited the rest of the island, the area around Samaná Bay was occupied by warlike Arawaks, sometimes called Carib indians. Their chieftain was a cacique named Cayapoa who dared to pay a personal visit to the ship of Columbus. His widow was baptized and known as Doña Ines Cayacos among the Spaniards.

Originally from South America, the Arawak Indians spoke an Amazonian dialect and they had migrated north through the Caribbean island chains to the island of Hispaniola. In spite of their warlike reputation the Arawaks were primarily farmers; they grew manioc and corn in fields that they cleared by burning off the jungle undergrowth. Arawak men hunted hutias (small rodents) and iguanas and spear fished in the island streams and in the ocean. Nevertheless the Arawaks had the honor of encountering the first Europeans to visit the Americas. On January 14, 1492, Christopher

Columbus attempted to land in beautiful Samaná Bay, but Columbus' men and an Arawak war party fought a brief skirmish, which was the first episode in a history of white — Indian wars, which would last almost 500 years. This occurred after the cacique Cayacoa returned to shore following his visit of the Spanish ship.

Above: bottom of the Samaná Bay.

When Columbus arrived at Samaná Bay, there were 1 million Arawaks. Thirteen years later there were only 60,000, and by 1533 these had been reduced to 6,000. By 1548 there were a scant 500, and when Sir Francis Drake raided Hispaniola in 1585 he reported that not one Arawak lived on the island. Part of the legacy of Christopher Columbus in Samaná can be found in the first name of the bay. The armed conflict between white conquistadors and native Indians was the reason why Columbus gave the name "Golfo de las flechas" (Bay of Arrows) to the present-day Samaná Bay.

There are rumors that the Samaná area was inhabited by "strange" white people centuries before Columbus sailed into the bay. There is a very interesting article in "Gazeta Oficial", number 366, from June 1881. A small archaeological expedition from France discovered ancient graves in a cave, locally known as "Cueva de San Gabriel". The local inhabitants also called it "Cueva de Infierno" (Cave of Hell). The head of the expedition confirmed that the skeletons definitely were not Indians. They were tall, about 180 cm, and the official conclusions were that these skeletons belonged to an unknown race. It seems that mysteries of Samaná have no end.

In 1523, Jean and Rouel Parmetier, two brothers from Dieppe, France, arrived in Samaná. They described the region as "una zona habitada por negros salvajes…", meaning that runaway African slaves inhabited the wildest and the most remote part of the peninsula. In 1643, Santo Domingo's governor, Antonio de Osorio, fearing that these slaves would incite other slaves to revolt and also to reduce the smuggling that was at its peak in the area, ordered an evacuation of the this zone and attacked the fugitive slaves. Just a year later the English tried to take possession of the peninsula, a task that they were not able to accomplish. Since French sailors were very frequent visitors of Samaná, many places received French names there. Some of them were later translated to Spanish. The peninsula was obviously very important for each of the nations that played a role in the New World. In 1673, Bertrand D´Obregon, governor of the pirate nest in Tortuga Island, attempted to establish a colony in Samaná by gathering all the dispersed inhabitants of the peninsula. He knew about this bay previously and when he fled from Puerto Rico after his raiding party of French buccaneers shipwrecked there, he sailed there immediately with the rest of his men. But he failed in his attempt and so he opted for a quick return to Tortuga where he assembled another huge group of sea rovers. A small group of the French established themselves in the bay anyway, supported by a group of Negro slaves that escaped from sugar and tobacco plantations on the island. Most of the inhabitants of Samaná were buccaneers and filibusters. The Spanish crown could not look at this foreign colony with favor and they ordered complete expulsion of the French colony in 1695.

In 1756, in order to prevent the French and the English from penetrating further into the island, the Spanish authorities brought a group of families from the Canary Islands to Hispaniola Island and they founded the oldest and largest city on the peninsula, called Santa Bárbara de Samaná, around 1760. Another group founded the town of Sabana del Mar in the southern part of the bay, meanwhile the French and the English continued their political and military maneuvering for control of this region. A few decades later with the Treaty of Basel in 1795, they traded the land off to Napoleon Bonaparte for some French-controlled territory back in Spain. France took possession of Hispaniola, including Samaná. The French had hoped to create a port in Samaná that would become the center of European imperial and colonial business in America. After the declaration of Haitian independence in 1804, Haitian military leaders took control of the entire island. After the independence of the Dominican Republic in 1844 the interest to dominate Samaná did not cease. The Americans came very close to buying the whole peninsula of Samaná. The contract was revoked at the last moment. The Americans wanted to build a naval base there. Many local residents speak English as a first language in Samaná and the US influence is also apparent in many of the last names of the settlers of this area. The consideration of building an American military base on the peninsula of Samaná came up again in the 1920s during American occupation of the island. One of the main reasons was to keep Germans from gaining a foothold there. (Today, the Germans are back in Samaná — along with French, Spanish, British, Swiss and other Europeans — as hotel and restaurant owners, and, of course, the tourists they cater to.)

Samaná was a very important harbor in the past. It is close to the deltas of the Yuna and Las Matas rivers where there was heavy shipping traffic bringing huge amounts of tobacco, sugar, leather and gold from the Santiago, La Vega and San Francisco de Macoris areas. These small vessels lightered in Samaná harbor where all the goods were loaded on board of big transatlantic ships that sailed with this cargo to the Spanish ports like Cádiz or Sevilla. Because of the coral reefs around and inside the Bay of Samaná there are literally hundreds of shipwrecks. It is not so surprising, considering that in 1700 there were more than 700 cargo ships transiting to and from the island during a single year. The bay has excellent conditions for navigation even though cargo ships cannot sail more than three miles into the bay because of mud in the shallows.

The sea bottom in the harbor is literally littered with an unimaginable number of artifacts from ships of all eras. Unfortunately, underwater research in the bay is restrained by sea conditions during most of the year; windy weather, murky water and sharks are the main obstacles.

Apart from this, Samaná and its surroundings always attracted many pirates seeking to bury parcels of their treasure there. Colonial-era pirates infested the area and plundered whichever ships were vulnerable at any given time. Until the 19th century a narrow channel separated the peninsula from the mainland, making it an ideal spot for the small pirate vessels to evade the larger Spanish galleons and French or British merchant ships and warships. Over time accumulations of sediment filled the channel and fused the island to the mainland, turning the former island into a peninsula, as we know it today.

After 1655 freebooters sailed the Caribbean waters generally with a corso patent, which was extended by one of the governors of the island of Tortuga or Jamaica, or any other Caribbean port where there was a seat of any European nation that was at war with Spain. Because of this "favor" given to the pirates, they had to pay one tenth of their booty to the above-mentioned governor. That was the reason why pirates always tried to lie about the real amount of their captured treasure in order avoid paying a large tax to the governor. To avoid this tribute, pirates buried part of their treasure on some of the many small cays that are strewn along the shores of the island of Hispaniola. Small deserted islands and cays in Samaná Bay, even small isolated beaches, were ideal places to hide booty. And it seems that our hero, Roberto Cofresí, was not an exception, especially taking into account that Samaná was his favorite region.

In contrast the inland portion of the peninsula is primarily wild. You find waterfalls and lush forests in the deep green mountains. A national park, Los Haitises, covering a huge area of 1,600 square kilometers, begins at the bottom of the Bay and it is home to dozens of endemic bird species, many reptiles and unique flora. Within the park, there are many hills and ravines, miles of wandering channels among the mangroves, which meet at occasional ponds and lakes. There are many caves in the area, some of which are host to petroglyphs let behind by the ancient Carib people.

Along with its beaches, Samaná may be best known for its world-class whale watching. This unique spectacle starts every year in the middle of January and ends two months later. The actual habitat of these whales is the North Atlantic Ocean. Every year in the winter season they come back to give birth and mate at the National Marine Mammals Sanctuary in Dominican waters, that covers an area from Silver Bank to the Bay of Samaná. Around 5,000 whales come here every January and stay for three to four months to feed their newborns until they are strong enough to bear the long journey northward in the open sea. Thousands of tourists from the world over come there each year, just to experience this unique natural spectacle.

The medallion

Some historians claim that Roberto Cofresí scuttled his ship full of treasure in front of Punta Gorda when he was cornered in Samaná Bay by Spanish ships. He allegedly escaped with his crew in a longboat to the nearby shallow mangroves. I also heard that several diving expeditions tried to find this sunken pirate ship, but always without success. In the past, the area was full of merchant ships that arrived here to load sugar cane, fruits, tobacco and other agricultural products originating in Cibao, the agricultural production area of the island, near its center. These products were transported here by riverboats.

Punta Gorda still exists and it is relatively close to the harbor in Sanchez, in the vicinity of a point of land just east of the town itself. Sanchez was originally called "Las Cañitas" and it's said that this village was founded by Roberto Cofresí or by his close friend, Joaquím Hernández. The fact that Sanchez was founded sometime around 1825, gives more credit to Hernández. I heard that Sanchez continues to be rife with stories about Cofresí, so I knew that I had to go there. I had a strange feeling that something might be waiting for me in this laid back village, about 30 kilometers from Santa Barbara de Samaná.

The primary road to Santa Barbara de Samaná goes through Sanchez, but the main part of this old town is to the right, towards the bay. It was raining... the rain drops were pounding the windshield of my old car when I turned to the right, heading to the harbor. Old wooden stakes with faded colors bordered the road and before long I was standing on the shore of Samaná Bay. To my right I could easily make out the dense mangroves that terminate the bay. Directly before me were the ruins of the old main pier, now rotting in the sun. Decades ago, Sanchez was a thriving harbor, but today, the only industry is the harvesting of shrimp that are so plentiful in these mangrove infested shallows.

I decided to make some inquiries. Under the wooden veranda of a nearby house there were three old men completely submersed in their game of dominos. I approached them and after few minutes they noticed a stranger watching them. They stopped playing and with polite smiles asked me what they could do for me. They invited me to sit down and I started to talk about local history, pirates, and Cofresí. The name, as I expected, was not strange to them at all. All three of them told me different stories, emphasizing of course, the sinking of the treasure boat of Cofresí in front of Sanchez. Eventually one of them suggested that I should talk to Antonio. Antonio turned out to be an old fisherman, living in a wooden cottage just a couple hundred meters from there. I thought that Antonio would give me another account of Roberto Cofresí's adventures around Samaná but when one of the domino players told me that Antonio wore a strange coin around his neck that was supposed to have belonged to Roberto Cofresí, my heart skipped a beat. But my informant laughed and told me in low tones to be cautious and patient, because Antonio is considered to be half crazy and nobody actually believed his story. I did not care about his warning; I just desperately wanted to see that coin. All three of them completely forgot their domino game and agreed to join me.

Walking along the shore, we arrived at Antonio's green cottage in a few minutes. Chickens wandered around the yard and three or four banana trees moved slowly in the light breeze. The rain had stopped. Two dogs began barking and finally a tall man with a sun and wind battered face emerged from the cottage. He was happy to see his three friends. Obviously they four of them were well acquainted. The trio explained the reason for my visit, with particular emphasis on Roberto Cofresí. Antonio sat down on an old, broken-down chair in the middle of his yard and stared skyward. The domino players could hardly restrain their laughter, while I scanned Antonio's chest, looking for some inkling of that "Cofresí coin". But, it was not possible to see anything beneath Antonio's woolen shirt.

We sat down in the small yard around him, and Antonio's daughter brought us cups of strong coffee. Antonio's green eyes pierced me. I explained to him that I was an historian looking for the treasures of Roberto Cofresí so that I might prove that legends are not always childish fairytales. He nodded and slowly put his right hand under the shirt and showed us a big silver coin with a small eyelet so that it could be used in the fashion of a pendant. The coin was hanging on a leather thong. He pulled it over his head and handed it to me. I must confess that my palms started to sweat as I gazed upon it. It was an old silver coin that I recognized, because I had seen a similar one some time ago. It was a type of silver 8 Reales coin, featuring the head of an Indian, and definitely a Colombian issue, though very damaged and worn. There were large letters REPUBLICA DE COLOMBIA around the faded Indian head and the date of 1820 was clearly seen under the bust. Despite being heavily worn, the date was still clear.

The coin was interesting, but with little numismatic value. However, the date of 1820 meant that it might be tied to Cofresí as he began his piracy about that time. Somehow, Cofresí was linked to the independence movement in Columbia in various legends originating with his life. The coin was punctured, possibly with a nail, toward its top, and a small silver wire was threaded through that hole, making it possible to hang the coin on a lanyard or necklace. But the reverse side took away my breath! The reverse side had been defaced completely and there were features etched upon it, as if a small map were depicted, along with some strange symbols. It was difficult to make out what was on the reverse side, but there were two letters engraved upon it toward the bottom of the coin: "RC".

I set out for home. Finally.

Antonio had explained to me that he got this coin/medallion from his grandfather many years ago. He was a fisherman, as had been all the men in the family for generations. Though he did not know with certainty where, when, or how his grandfather got this unique piece, he obtained it somewhere in the area of Samaná. As Antonio recalled, his dad and his grandpa never traveled beyond the bay; they sailed the bay in their small fishing yola almost every day. He also added, with some sadness, that nobody believed him. He did not care. He wore this coin/medallion to remind him of his father and grandfather.

I knew that this was the opportunity of a lifetime. I must try to convince Antonio to sell me the medallion. It was a difficult task but I was willing to hang in there until I got it. Actually, it did take long to arrive at an acceptable deal. Antonio, the father of six children, preferred to have some cash in his pocket rather than the old medallion around his neck. So we finally shook hands, drank some cold Presidente beers and I happily left with the medallion in hand. I could not wait to get home and seriously investigate the engravings on the reverse side of the coin. The year of mint, 1820, perfectly matched the period when Roberto Cofresí was busy looting merchant ships around Samaná Bay. And I was absolutely sure that the lines and symbols were some kind of treasure map.

I sat down at the kitchen table, and started to examine the engravings. There were portions almost obliterated after so many years of wear. There was a rendering of a mountain with a cave, and in front of this cave there were some tiny lines, which could represent ocean waves. Below the waves there was definitely a chain! The famous Cofresí chain! On the left side there was an arrow pointing to the sun on the right side of the cave. There was also one palm tree, or it could be an "x" on a pole? Beneath that there was a symbol that I could not decipher at all. I was sure there was the letter "A" on one side but the symbol itself was some kind of a half circle and horizontal line above it. Below the chain there were two letters, "RC".

There was no barrel, which — according to all the legends about the medallions or Cofresí treasure maps — there was always a barrel present on the treasure engravings. But there was a chain and the letters "RC".

I tried cleaning the reverse side of the coin displaying the engravings with a soft cloth. I managed to remove most of the dirt and some

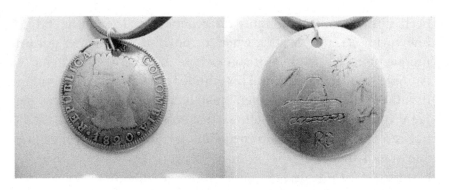

Above: the medallion's reverse and obverse featuring a map and bearing the initials "RC".

black crust, but the engravings were now even less visible without the soiled contrast. So I took a sharp nail and began very cautiously to enhance the engraved lines in order to make them more visible. When I finished, I cleaned the whole surface again and now it was much clearer than before. I closely examined the whole reverse side to be certain that I did not miss anything. Now I was satisfied. The second step was to find out which cave Cofresí meant in particular. I was sure that it must be one of the caves found along the shores of the Samaná peninsula, not necessarily those in the national park of Los Haitises. And I even thought that I might know which one.

But my euphoria soon faded, replaced by doubt. Not about the place where I wanted to go, but I was not sure if I would be able to find the treasure using only a metal detector and shovel. The search area was not large, but there could be stones, layers of natural sediment, and who knows what else that might obstruct me. And I knew that I could not camp there for any period of time because that would definitely attract curious locals, sooner or later.

But I had to give it a try.

Jorge Traveira

I was in a bad mood. So many locations and zero results. It seemed to me that rumors and metal detectors are simply not enough to pull off a successful search. While in this depressed funk, I got a message from a friend of mine asking if he could give my phone number to his partner in Portugal. His name was Jorge Traveira and he was not only a treasure hunter, but also some kind of scientist who was supposed to have developed some kind of electronic unit, which can positively locate gold and diamonds under dry land or in the ocean. Jorge was interested in coming to the Dominican Republic with all his equipment and his team to search for the infamous pirate ship, the *Golden Fleece*. My friend knew that I had research regarding this shipwreck so he thought that I would be an ideal contact for Jorge.

Golden Fleece sank in the Bay of Samaná in 1686 during a fierce naval battle with two British war frigates. The captain of *Golden Fleece* was the English privateer Jack Bannister. He lost his ship, but he managed to escape aboard a smaller vessel into the mangrove channels at the bottom of the bay where the British frigates could not follow him. But the luck of Jack Bannister did not last too long. He was caught just a few months later and hanged on the mast. *Golden Fleece*, still loaded with booty lies under the layer of sand on the bottom of the bay. And I was sure that I knew the exact position of this treasure wreck. And I mean the REAL position, not one that was claimed by other treasure hunters. And unlike these other folks, I possessed the hard evidence and proof.

Golden Fleece was in Samaná Bay, and most of the treasures of Cofresí were supposed to be buried in this area too, so it seemed to me like the perfect opportunity. I was sure that I could convince Jorge to look for the pirate treasure buried on land as well. If his electronic units were so accurate, it could mean a timely success. The day I talked to Jorge on the phone I found him to be an enthusiastic man, devoted to his hobby of treasure hunting. As I understood it, this was not merely a hobby, but more like a regular line of work for him. We made an agreement on terms in short order, and Jorge expressed his interest in searching for the Cofresí treasures on the land as well. But, of course, first the *Golden Fleece*. I agreed.

Within two weeks Jorge notified me that he had purchased tickets and would be on his way to the Dominican Republic with his son and his nephew. His son, Pedro, and his nephew, Joao were experts in the use of the electronic equipment Jorge used for the hunt. This was perfectly fine with me as the entire team was of a single family. Finally they arrived at the Las Americas airport outside Santo Domingo. I had mixed emotions as I viewed the Iberian Airbus taxi across the tarmac. Could these people actually help me in my treasure quest? Only time could tell.

Above: the Bannister Hotel.

My first impressions of Jorge, Pedro and Joao gave me a good feeling. The quantity of equipment they brought with them, packed in huge black containers raised my hopes. Jorge paid a great deal in freight charges to get the equipment here.

They were quite tired, having flown from their home town of Coimbra to Puerto, from Puerto to Madrid, and then from Madrid to Santo Domingo. But even so, on the way to their hotel we eager to discuss our plans and strategies for the hunt. The future looked bright for me once more.

The following day we agreed that the equipment should be properly calibrated. I am not a technician, so elaborating on magnetic north versus polar declinations, degrees of difference, sending various frequency waves and then lapse periods of agitated electron response for individual mineral and metal elements, was beyond me, but they seemed to be pretty sure of themselves. We decided to move to Samaná and visit a beach first, to try out the equipment and prepare it for an actual mission. I was happy. We left early in the morning and my old, but reliable Chevy Tahoe 2005 was fully load-

Above: Jorge Traveira.

ed, maybe overloaded. Myself, Jorge, Joao and Pedro plus the heavy boxes, metal detectors, diving equipment and luggage of all the sizes filled my car completely. We passed by busy Santo Domingo and entered a new highway going to the peninsula of Samaná. Five hours later we finally saw the huge stone sign for Puerto Bahia. After driving several hundred meters through the trees and carefully trimmed grass fields down to the ocean we stopped in front of the place where we would be staying for the next few days — the Bannister Hotel.

I must say that the hotel is luxurious and beautiful. It has a fully equipped marina that was filled with huge sailboats and catamarans. We got our rooms, and agreed to leave early in the morning to a beach known as Playa El Valle. It is on the opposite side of the peninsula, close to the famous Playa Rincon. The reason why I chose this beach for testing of all of Jorge's electronic equipment was that I knew about a shipwreck sunk off the shore that was supposed to contain gold. The wreck was almost completely buried under the sandy bottom, so it was an ideal target for Jorge to prove his devices worked. Of course, I did not tell them where the wreck rests; they had to find it. That was the purpose of the test. We discussed all the potentialities of the hunt over a huge lobster lunch, deliciously prepared on the beach, and I could tell that Jorge was a true Portuguese — a lover of good food. We really had a good time but I could not understand how absolutely certain Jorge and his boys were that they would find "my" wreck in less than in two hours, simply doing their measurements from the shore.

Chapter Four

Samaná beaches

Samaná peninsula has several small beaches, frequently bordered with cliffs and rocks. The only exception is the famous Playa Rincon, considered to be one of the most beautiful beaches in the world. Before proceeding to Cayo Levantado and the small keys at the bottom of the bay, and especially before we headed for the caves in the mangroves, I decided — just in case — to quickly explore these beaches, at least those beaches which Roberto Cofresí positively visited. I knew that most of them were now public beaches, frequented by many visitors on weekends, but also during the week because they were very close to the actual town of Santa Barbara de Samaná. Subsequently the possibility of finding some treasure evidence there was almost zero. But one has to try.

The first beach we went to, and the closest one to town, is Playa Anandel. Roberto Cofresí anchored his ship in front of this beach many times. He went there on land to visit his relatives. Two hundred years ago it was still quite isolated and not close to the town's residential area. Today, the story is completely different. Playa Anandel is practically part of the suburbs of Santa Barbara de Samaná. There are permanent cottages surrounding it and there are even some rus-

Above: Playa Anandel as seen from the main road.

tic restaurants and gift shops. The main road passes by less than a hundred meters from the shore. And lots of garbage. If there was some buried Cofresí treasure, we would not find it today.

I continued onward, passing more small sandy beaches, a few of them having small rocky islands offshore, however the road was still lined with houses and the beaches were covered with fishing nets and yolas.

The farther I drove away from town, the fewer the houses, but there were still some along the road. As I passed Puerto Carenero I recalled that some of the historical documents I had read indicated that this was the place where ships had been careened in the past.

Even the infamous pirate Blackbeard supposedly came here for this reason. Finally we arrived at Punta Balandra. It was over ten kilometers from the town itself but the area was still heavily populated. On the right side there is a luxury private resort, the Vista Mare. I knew from the map and from the archives that there should be a beach surrounded with rocks where Cofresí was known to have

Above: small beach close to Puerto Carenero.

landed at least once. It was already afternoon. I had planned to stay overnight in the area anyway, and my wife and kids were with me this time, so I decided to stay there overnight and use the time to explore the beach using my Fisher Pulse metal detector.

The beach is private (though this is not officially allowed in the Dominican Republic) and belongs to the resort. Only members or paying guests are allowed to go there and a permanent resort guard is on duty there as well. The beach was completely deserted with huge waves crashing against the rocky walls that surrounded it. I walked over the fine sand, my feet washed by water and I imagined how it was at this place 200 years ago. The pirate ship *Ana* might have been at anchor in the bay and I could almost see the tall figure of Roberto Cofresí standing firmly on the bow of the boat watching over his crew.

Since nobody was there, I took out my metal detector and I started searching around the rocks that stretched into the water. After an hour of intensive search the only result was an iron cable and a long

Above: a private beach in Vista Mare close to Punta Balandra.
Below: a view of Cayo Levantado from Vista Mare.

nail covered with fine coral fragments. The rocks had no odd formations; there was no single old tree to be seen, so there seemed to be nothing here that would induce a pirate to bury treasure.

Back on the top of the small hill overlooking the property, I could enjoy the view of the whole bay. The famous Cayo Levantado, my next target, was just in view before me, sitting quietly less than two

Above: Playa Rincon.
Below: western end of Playa Rincon near the cold creek.

kilometers from our viewpoint. The last visitors had already left the island and it looked empty from this distance. I knew that there was a luxury hotel, Bahia Principe, on the opposite side of Cayo Levantado. This hotel does not accept children and the only way to get there is by way of the hotel water taxi. The hotel property is strictly separated from the public beach on the other side of the island.

Next morning we set out for the famous beach known as Playa Rincon. It's not only famous on the Samaná peninsula, it is known worldwide as one of the most beautiful beaches on the planet.

A prime destination of tourist, the place has that feel and appearance. Three kilometers of white sand bordered with hundreds of palm trees with a magnificent view of the large bay surrounded by steep hills full of coconut palms is really impressive. On both sides of the beach there are tourist establishments, shops and restaurants.

On the western side of the Rincon there is creek that empties into the bay. There are several shops and bars there as well. A fisherman told me that some time ago several silver coins were found on a sandy patch on the corner of the beach, but in despite my best efforts, I could find out nothing more about this discovery. No sense in using a metal detector here; under the sand there are dozens of beer caps and nails. The beach is a pleasant natural feature itself, but not a location conducive to a treasure hunt. We struck out.

On the way back I passed by another small beach, called Playa Colorada. In Cofresí history "Caño Colorado", which means "colored stream", was mentioned several times as a waterway used by Roberto Cofresí on several occasions as an escape route. Today, Playa Colorada is small, public beach with a few coconut palms and lots of trash everywhere.

Cayo Levantado

I've already mentioned this island in previous chapters of this book. The original name of this key, together with two small rocky islands on the west and east, were "Cayos Rebeldes", or "Cayos Bannister", in honor of a great naval battle between two English war frigates and the pirate ship of Jack Bannister, the famous Golden Fleece. The pirate ship caught fire and sank in 4 fathoms of water. It lies there still.

This sandy key covered with vegetation was a favorite careening location for a number of pirates. There were two other careening locations closer to the town of Santa Barbara de Samaná, but these places could not be approached by a vessel of any size. These additional locations are known as "Carenero Grande" and "Carenero Chiquito" (Big Careen and Small Careen).

Cayo Levantado is the largest of the three keys. It's about 930 meters long, about .4 kilometers square, with an elevation of 26 meters above sea level. The second key, Cayo Farola is just a rocky outcrop covered with small bushes, about 200 meters long, and it is about 400 meters from Cayo Levantado. The third, Cayo Arena, is nothing more than a rock barely above sea level.

Cayo Levantado was definitely visited several times by Roberto Cofresí and therefore there was a good chance that he might have buried some of his treasure on this tiny island. Theoretically it was possible — the island, fairly distant from Santa Barbara, was covered with trees and vegetation. In other words, it was worth exploring.

Half of Cayo Levantado is public and the other half is private, belonging to the five star hotel Bahia Principe Cayo Levantado. You can find a boat in Samana's harbor that will take you to the public side at any time of the day. The ride takes about 25 minutes. A short paved sidewalk through the trees took us to the beach, which was, in my opinion, overcrowded. The place is over run with tourists from local hotels, day-trippers, and passengers of luxury Caribbean cruises. Dozens of small booths offering photos with parrots, and carryout food border the tree-lined beach. There is no privacy here. Our boat was scheduled to return to the mainland in four hours, leaving me some time to explore. A strange rock at the eastern end of the beach drew my immediate attention. It looked like a cannon ball hit the rock and passed through it. It was most probably the result of the previously mentioned naval battle between the British and Jack Bannister. But this rock could be an ideal demark for somebody who wanted to hide some treasure here. If it was Roberto Cofresí, the rock was already there, because the naval battle occurred in 1686 and our pirate hero visited Cayo Levantado between 1822 and 1825.

I knew from my previous investigations that there is a huge difference between low tide and high tide on Cayo Levantado. This fluctuation is caused by very shallow water around the beach and a wide

Above: peculiar rock formation on the public beach at Cayo Levantado.

band of sand is always exposed during low tide. Therefore it was also an ideal spot to careen ships. At low tide the rock is almost fully exposed. My problem was that the touring hours on the island were only between 8 am and 4 pm. Tide changes early in the morning and late in the evening. At those hours there are only guards on the beach. The investigation of this place would take some time. If there were no people around and you had sufficient time to use a metal detector you still would be harried with bottle caps, cans and other metal trash and garbage. Anyway, at that instant, it was not realistic to begin a search. So I spent the rest of our visit on Cayo Levantado imagining that I could see Roberto Cofresí jumping out of his long-boat with a small chest on his shoulder and shovel in hand.

Preciosa Beach

Roberto Cofresí is alleged to have frequently visited the beaches of Playa Grande, Playa Preciosa and Playa Diamante, all being east of the small, northern coastal town of Rio San Juan. A new road connects Puerto Plata with Nagua and Samaná, so the trip was much quicker and safer than it was a couple of years ago.

I passed Souse and Cabarete, arriving at Rio San Juan on an asphalt road where I found a sign reading: "Public Beach". The road then led to a huge public parking lot where there were some cars, tourist buses and a number of kiosks offering food and drink at the beachfront. This was the famous Playa Grande beach and it was full of people, as I had expected. This was not exactly the place I was looking for. There was a nice paved path leading to the east from the parking lot. I walked a few meters and stopped. I could not believe my eyes. Paradise lay before me! I was looking at a white, sandy

Below: the author on Preciosa beach.

beach, completely empty, without any sign of humans, caressed with crystal clear water. The beach, about 800 meters in length, ended with a rocky cliff. Yes, it was the place I was looking for — Playa Preciosa.

I knew from my earlier investigation that this beach was something special. The US based treasure hunting company, Deep Blue Marine, discovered one of the oldest shipwrecks in the Caribbean near here. They recovered hundreds of Spanish coins dating from around 1550, Mayan jade figurines, and other valuable artifacts. It is highly possible that the shipwreck could be the famous Spanish treasure galleon *San Miguel*. Most of her cargo remains under the sandy bottom of the bay. There is another shipwreck here, a large iron cargo ship. A section of her corroded boilers protrudes from the water on low tide and can be clearly seen from a distance. Some say that it was a German ship that sank in the bay around 1943. After Deep Blue divers recovered an American whiskey bottle and a shoe made in the USA, they were sure it was an American cargo ship. I do not know why, but this shipwreck intrigued me. I asked a local tourist guide what he knew about this shipwreck and without any hesitation he claimed that it was a huge Chinese ship full of tractors and trucks that sank more than hundred years ago. No comment....

After assembling my Tesoro Sand Shark (metal detector), I stepped onto the soft sand and began my search at the base of a coconut palm. I was completely alone in this small piece of paradise; there was absolutely no one there. I walked slowly till I reached the end of the beach where it abruptly ended with a cliff. No hits. This was strange because I expected to find, at least, some garbage left behind by the tourists. I spied no particularly impressive rock formations, but there was a huge tree several dozen meters from the beach that attracted my attention. So I put my metal detector to work and started to search the area.

I checked the area around the tree without success. When I was ready to switch my detector off, I heard a faint signal. Let's see. I started to dig. The sand ended and dark, harder soil began. I excavated a hole almost 30 centimeters deep and the signal was louder. Finally, a piece of metal appeared in the bottom of the hole. It looked like brass. I pulled it out and checked it over. There were letters and

Above: the author detecting at Preciosa beach

numbers engraved on it. It was evidently old, but not 200 years old. As per routine, I checked the bottom of the hole again with my metal detector. I expected nothing, because I presumed I had found my target, but to my surprise another loud sound came through my headphones. So I dug a little deeper and another brass artifact appeared. This time it was some sort of metal label with faded engravings.

I cleaned it and using magnifying glass, I could clearly read the words "DETROIT RADIATOR LUBRICATOR" and the year "1905". Clearly, both of these brass plates belonged to the iron ship in the bay. Mystery solved. It was definitely an American ship. Unfortunately, this was only a pleasant distraction that had nothing to do with my primary target — the treasure of Roberto Cofresí.

On return to the beach entrance I stopped at an odd concrete bunker of some sort featuring a roof and standing walls. There was an old fisherman there cleaning his catch, so I asked him what exactly this construction might be.

He told me that the locals built it during the Second World War and the purpose was to cover their speedboats from curious onlookers. These boats were supposedly used for secret deliveries of fresh supplies to German U-boats during the second half of the war, when the infamous "gray wolves" began operating in the Caribbean, harassing US convoys. I knew this to be a fact and that the beaches around Playa Grande were indeed used for this purpose. Long ago I had talked to an old lady, who had a restaurant in Sosua, and she delivered cheese and fresh meat to the German U-boat crews on a regular basis. She told me that they paid her in gold coins. The same fisherman also told me that the iron ship in the bay was an old cargo ship that ran aground in 1923 on the coral reef in heavy fog. I do not know where he got this information, but it made sense to me.

The story was interesting, but unfortunately it had nothing to do with the treasure of Roberto Cofresí. So I had to put another black cross on my list of possible places where some of his treasure could be buried. Well, life goes on, but I had to admit that my perseverance and patience also had limits.

The treasure

Study of the medallion, coupled with my previous collection of maps and associated information gave me assurance that I had, in fact, previously visited one of the caves depicted on the medallion. The medallion, in my opinion would not lie to me and I had no doubt as to its authenticity. I simply could not understand why somebody else had not been curious enough to investigate further after all these years, considering that the medallion was widely known to be a Cofresí artifact, designed specifically as a map. I still could not believe my luck.

I am aware that many entries in Wikipedia are posted without any factual support, but I could not resist re-reading, on numerous occasions, one special entry in the Roberto Cofresí subject page regarding the mysterious medallion: *"Other accounts list other distinctions, including a series of silver medallions engraved with the initials 'R.C.', or a chain that emerged from the sea and went into the jungle. Throughout the Dominican Republic, there are supposedly nearly 30 locations where loot was buried along (with) these medallions, most of which remain undiscovered."*

I was sure I had prepared myself well for my final step of this quest. After the successful tests of Jorge's equipment in Playa del Valle where the devices proved to be so effective in searching for gold, I believed we should find a Cofresí stash in a day, perhaps less. After returning to the hotel from Playa del Valle, we agreed on a plan regarding a Cofresí treasure find, and how to proceed. I knew that Roberto Cofresí generally did not bury his treasures too deep in the ground, so I expected that this target would not be an exception; even though 200 years of sediment and calcification would definitely have some effect on the recovery. There could be mudslides, rock falls, sediments, and layers of rotting vegetation that mitigated the actual depth of the burial. I hung the Cofresí medallion around my neck and we set off. The treasure was waiting for us....

I remembered my first trip to the cave area in the Los Haitises National Park a few weeks back. I decided to go there via the eastern part of Samaná Bay, an area with endless white beaches, coconut palms, with small rivers and streams pouring into the sea. The main towns in the area are Mitches and Sabana de la Mar. Both are fishing villages and a small ferry leaves twice a day from Santa Barbara de Samaná in route to a pier in Sabana de la Mar. But I had another reason to visit Mitches: the river that empties into the sea near the town's public beach, is supposedly where a fisherman found a coffer full of golden jewelry and coins on the exposed sandy bottom after some heavy rains. No doubt it was a Roberto Cofresí cache because the fisherman found it in the area where legend claims Cofresí buried it. I described the fate of the treasure and of the fisherman previously in this book. Our pirate was definitely very active in this region and specifically in this locale bordering the Los Haitises National Park, which is full of caves, rivers, streams and mangrove channels.

We drove to the public beach and made inquiries of some old men who were sitting there in the shade playing dominos. They remembered the story and showed me the spot, very close to the sea, where the treasure was found. Sixty years ago the stream was much smaller than today, and there were no houses around, only the dense jungle.

The specific cave that I had in mind was also on Samaná peninsula, but not found amongst the mangrove channels of the National Park. This was fortunate because we would not require the use of a boat, as had been the case several weeks earlier when I had used one from Sabana de la Mar. The cave I had in mind was close to the beach, but still a little difficult to reach.

I dreaded lugging all the necessary equipment through the dense jungle, but there was no other option. Apart from the electronic equipment, we had to carry metal detectors, shovels and other digging tools. We did not know the condition of the soil there. In the evening I convinced Jorge and his team to spend one day looking for "my" treasure before we went looking for *Golden Fleece*. They agreed.

The next morning it was cloudy and windy, but it suited us, unless it started raining. We quickly packed all our stuff in the car, and on the way through town we bought some provisions for the day and followed the road until it became impassable. At that point we unpacked everything, divided the boxes and rucksacks among the four

of us and headed into the jungle. I knew that the cave was not far, close to a small creek near a rocky beach.

We were using a machete to cut our way through dense vegetation and after about half an hour we arrived at the entrance of the small cave. Nobody had been there for a long time. It was obvious. And I said to myself — now or never.

Jorge and Joao immediately started setting up their equipment. It was apparent to me that they were good team and that they definitely had done this before. They each knew what to do, and when to do it. I stood by, ready with my metal detector and shovel.

Joao broadcast his frequency waves from one corner and then from the other corner of the small opening in front of the cave. There was a tension in the air you could cut with a knife. We sere so immersed in the quest at this point that the passing hours slipped by without notice.

It took Joao, Pedro and Jorge over two hours to perform all the measurements. The data was collected in a computer, latitude and longitude double checked, and I could see the lines in the computerized map crossing one point in the front of the entrance. Joao went to that point with his metal wands and I saw how they violently

crossed in front of his chest at the same location indicated on the map depicted by the computer. Unbelievable!

We gathered at the marked spot with our metal detectors. It was not long before the detectors started to sing. Now the shovels. We only had two small shovels and the soil was a little hard, so the digging was difficult. We were sweating, but forgot our hunger and thirst as we worked under the intense tropical sun. We did not care. Our eyes were only focused on the bottom of the hole we were digging. Periodically we checked the excavation with a metal detector

and the sound was always stronger with increasing pitch. There was something big down there!

When the shovel finally hit something hard, we all froze for a moment. Then we started to dig in a frenzy, even using our bare hands. Finally, the old wooden lid of a small box appeared before our eyes. It was dark brown, full of scratches and dirt, but it looked to me like the most beautiful chest I'd ever seen! We decided we should not remove the chest, even though it was not very big. The clock was working against us. Four gringos loaded with strange equipment would certainly draw the attention of the local people and we suspected that we might have some curious visitors at any moment. And that was exactly what we did not need. We only cleared away enough dirt from the edges of the chest so that we might slip a knife under the lid. We then pried upward, hoping to overcome the rusted iron lock, but it did not want to give way, resisting our efforts to discover what lay beneath. Finally the 200-year-old wood gave up and the chest opened with a bang. We stared into the chest. It was there! I looked around and I could feel the spirit of Roberto Cofresí, the Black Prince of the Caribbean, staring down at us from above.

I bowed to the invisible spirit of the Last Pirate of the Caribbean. In my own mind I gave him many thanks as I glanced round at the smiling faces of my friends.

Epilogue

Many legends and myths about Roberto Cofresí, his adventures, and hidden treasure persist, especially in the areas of the island he was known to frequent.

Cofresí aficionados agree that at least some of these legends — if not many — might be true, despite the fact that there is not much in the way evidence to support them. The verifiable information is generally found in military reports, or comes to us via the Spanish archives in Puerto Rico and Santo Domingo, contemporary articles, relatives of Cofresí, his associates who evaded Spanish authorities, and from some books authored by a few serious historians who studied the pirate and made their research public.

Unfortunately there are not many serious books or written reports about the life of Roberto Cofresí. But all the accessible historical documents, and serious books define him as a public hero, stealing from the rich and giving to the poor. Only one investigator from Puerto Rico, Walter Cardona Bonet, defines Roberto Cofresí differently — he describes him in his book "El Marinero, Bandolero, Pirata y Contrabandista Roberto Cofresí" (Sailor, Bandit, Pirate and Smuggler Roberto Cofresí), published in San Juan, Puerto Rico, in 1991, as a ruthless pirate killing for pleasure and money, who also stole from farmers and merchants on land. But I find this very doubtful. Cofresí was, without question, a pirate. He was surely sometimes forced to kill. He was also driven by anger in some cases, when, for example, his close friends were killed in ambush, but generally speaking, he was not a ruthless person who killed for the sake of killing regardless. Even so, there is a claim by some that Roberto Cofresí killed between 300 and 400 persons during his raids and pirate adventures on the high seas. The truth is that he was called "The Terror of the Caribbean" by authorities. Any way you cut it, good or bad, he was a person who rebelled against the rules and he was a local hero of the inhabitants of Puerto Rico and Hispaniola Island (today's Dominican Republic and Haiti). Proof of this can be found in the city of Boquerón.

There are not many countries in the world that would pay tribute and honor to a pirate but they have done it in Puerto Rico. A large statue of Roberto Cofresí was erected at the spa in the bay of Boquerón in 1991. Jose Buscaglia Guillermety sculpted it and this statue clearly shows how the people of Puerto Rico have always appreciated their hero.

Above: Statue of Roberto Cofresí at the entrance of the spa in Boquerón, Cabo Rojo, Puerto Rico. Courtesy Wiki Commons

Most authors and historians writing about Roberto Cofresí describe him as a tall, strong man with piercing blue eyes, blond hair and handsome face. Later in time he had a blond beard. His piercing eyes showed determination, courage and intelligence. He must have contrasted dramatically with the dark skin and black eyes of the natives and Spaniards living in Puerto Rico at that time. All his biographers define him as being extremely brave. He was always the first one to board the ship, ax in one hand and pistol in the other. His crew loved him, respected him and all were willing to die for him. The following recollection, has been confirmed by several authors: during a fierce shipboard battle, one of the combatants pointed a rifle at Roberto's back, but one of Roberto's faithful pirate fellows, Galache, who was his pilot, jumped into the line of fire and was subsequently shot. He was killed but his beloved captain was saved.

Stories claiming that Cofresí nailed his prisoners on the deck of his ship are pure nonsense, as are those that claim he scuttled the ships he looted and let the crew drown. On the contrary, the majority of persons writing about Roberto Cofresí emphasize his generosity. It has been said repeatedly that Roberto Cofresí became a pirate, not because of his character, but because of the political situation at the time that left him subjugated and in want. He was not an assassin. When he killed anyone it was always in battle, never for pure entertainment. He was, no doubt, a very intelligent person, in spite of the fact that he had no higher education. His parents took him out of school when he was thirteen simply because they did not have enough money to support him. It's said that he always spared the lives of children, women, and the elderly.

There are many stories about his gifts to poor fishermen on the coast both of Hispaniola and Puerto Rico, and it is commonly known that he shared his booty with the poor people of both nations. Therefore they were willing to help him anytime and anywhere. Many fishermen served him as spies, watching the comings and goings of merchant ships and passed that valuable information on to him. Nestor Rodriguez Escudero related how Cofresí saved a young girl from a ship he'd just attacked. He left her in a small town called Yauco with Father Pieretti, a catholic priest, covering all her expenses until she was returned to her family. Another story says that Cofresí protected another young girl named Adela whom an old pirate entrusted to him as a daughter as he was dying from wounds received during the capture of a ship. Two other authors, Francisco Ortea and Alejandro Tapia, wrote that Roberto Cofresí risked his life to save an infant. And he left a small boy with another catholic priest, Father Antonio, who returned him to his relatives along with a "good sum of money".

Roberto was attracted to the sea and to ships from early childhood. Many times he did not go to school but spent the day instead in his small rowboat, dreaming about distant horizons and sea adventures. The late 1700s and early 1800s were very turbulent times for the Spanish Crown. Many of its former colonies, such as Puerto Rico, Hispaniola, Mexico, and Cuba had begun establishing their own cultural identities, especially after slavery was abolished. These colonies began demanding their independence from Spain and Spanish naval forces found themselves occupied fighting Simon Bolivar in Venezuela. Under this threat the Spanish government began removing their gold and silver from these colonies, anticipating their separation through revolution.

Roberto Cofresí was a logical product of these turbulent times. Seas around his native Puerto Rico and Hispaniola were full of merchant ships with gold and silver on board and there were corsair and pirate ships as well. The lure of easy bounty that could be taken from these ships was one of the reasons why he opted for his pirate career. Another reason was, according to several authors, a slap in the face by an English Captain. Some historians even consider Roberto Cofresí a patriot, a man who was the first to oppose the expansive maritime policies of foreign nations, thereby defending independence of Puerto Rico. We know that Cofresí visited the coast of Venezuela many times, and there is even a theory based on some old testimony and documents that Roberto Cofresí personally helped Simon Bolívar. Some authors even claim that Cofresí sailed the waters of the Caribbean with the revolutionary flag of Gran Colombia. There are authors who claim that during Cofresí's last battle at sea his ship was flying the flag of the Republic of Colombia, but this has never been confirmed.

Roberto Cofresí was the greatest pirate of his era in the entire Caribbean. Yes, there were some lesser freebooters in the Caribbean as well, such as Charles Gibbs, Samuel Hall Lord, and Mansel Alcantra, but these pirates were hardly comparable.

Cofresí possessed extraordinary courage. Francisco Ortea wrote:

"for his boldness and courage, he (Cofresí) was worthy of a better occupation and fate". He is alleged to severely punish his crew for not showing proper respect for women, children and elderly persons on several occasions. Roberto Cofresí's generosity, geniality, courage, and chivalry won him many friends and admirers. We know that he organized his own espionage service. Some authors mention some of his spies such as, for example, in Ponce, a rural teacher, in Mayaguez, a canteen waitress, and in the town of Arecibo, there was a priest. All his spies were monitoring not only the movement of merchant ships but, most importantly, civil guard and military activities. When Cofresí and ten members of his crew were captured in Guayama, many people from surrounding towns went there and gathered in front of the jail hoping to see him.

There are still many mysteries surrounding Cofresí´s death. There are two official versions regarding his final capture; one is Spanish and the other is an American version. There are also discrepancies in details regarding his execution by firing squad. What is certain is the fact that he and his crew were judged by a military court and not by a civil court.

As I wrote on the first page of this book — the legends should be believed, followed and investigated. If done seriously, this is always a difficult job, tiresome and time consuming. It is a test of your strength and perseverance, but in this case, the discovery of treasure made it all worthwhile.

Author

Bibliography

CAMACHO, Luis Asencio ...Corsario

CARDONA, Bonet Walter ...El Marinero, Bandolero, Pirata y Contrabandista Roberto Cofresí (1819-1825)

COOPER, Lee ...The Pirate of Puerto Rico

FERRERAS, Ramon Alberto ...Cofresí, el Intrépido

GONZÁLES, Geraldino ...Riquezas Dominicanas: Islas,Cayos e Islotes de la República Dominicana

KORDAC, Lubos ...Hidden and Lost Treasures in the Dominican Republic

KORDAC, Lubos ...Historic Shipwrecks of the Dominican Republic and Haiti

MARTIN, Arsenio ...Isla de Mona es Isla de Tesoros

MECTEL, Angelika ...Das Kurge Heldenhafte Leben Des Don Roberto Cofresí
TAPIA, Rivera Alejandro ...Cofresí

VALLEDOR, Roberto Fernandez ...El Mito de Cofresí en la Narrativa Antillana

VAZQUEZ, Edwin ...El Bravo Pirata de Puerto Rico

Local Dominican newspapers and magazines

Internet sources

Place Index

Made in United States
North Haven, CT
09 August 2022

22504764R00088